THE MORALITY OF BUSINESS

A Profession for Human Wealthcare

THE MORALITY OF BUSINESS

A Profession for Human Wealthcare

Tibor R. Machan

Argyros School of Business & Economics
Chapman University, USA

 Springer

Library of Congress Control Number: 2006935655

ISBN-13: 978-0-387-48906-3   ISBN-13: 978-0-387-48907-0 (e-book)
ISBN:10: 0-387-48906-1   ISBN:10: 0-387-48907-X (e-book)

Printed on acid-free paper.

Printed in the United States of America.

9 8 7 6 5 4 3 2 1

springer.com

"I was coming back from Africa on one of my trips, . . . I had taken one of my wealthy friends with me. She said, 'Don't you just feel guilty? Don't you just feel terrible?' I said, 'No, I don't. I do not know how my being destitute is going to help them.' Then I said when we got home, 'I'm going home to sleep on my Pratesi sheets right now and I'll feel good about it.' "

Oprah Winfrey, speaking in Baltimore on 04/10/06 at a fund-raiser for Beth Tfiloh Dahan Community School

CONTENTS

ACKNOWLEDGEMENTS

Thanks are due to Judith Myers, David M. Brown, Donald Booth, Joe Cobb, and Jim Chesher for editorial help. Dave and Judy Thresher, who endowed the R. C Hoiles Chair I hold at Chapman University, are responsible for some of the financial support that made this work possible, and I am grateful to them for that support. Material in this work has been drawn from some of my columns written for Freedom News Wires, the *Notre Dame Journal of Law and Public Politics*, and the *Journal of Value Inquiry*.

Chapter 1

INTRODUCTION
A Brief On Business Ethics

Why worry about the nature of business – its ethical underpinnings and its reputation, its most common format the business corporation or enterprise or company? Because, for those of us bent on living well, this is a vital profession, comparable to medicine or nutrition, since it produces prosperity for people. Professionals here, no less than in those lines of work, aim for something that's good for many of us.[1] So it matters that they act decently, with professional integrity. It matters that they don't fall prey to the temptation to deceive, cheat, or lie, just as it matters that physicians remain above-board and refuse to become charlatans and quacks.

It has long been held, however, that the accumulation of wealth is not really a good pursuit, only something instrumentally worthwhile. Thomas Aquinas put it this way:

> For wealth is not sought except for the sake of something else: because of itself it brings us no good, but only when we use it, whether for the support of the body, or for some similar purposes. Now the supreme good is sought for its own, and not for another's sake. Therefore wealth is not man's supreme good.[2]

Yet all this could be said as confidently about health or education or science – none of these are the supreme good, at least not as Aquinas would define it: the life of pure contemplation, following the example of Aristotle. Yet they could, as could wealth, be constitutive of the supreme good: a life that is well-lived, successful and happy.

The first consideration in our discussion of wealth, then, is how to carry it off decently, that is to say, business ethics. These are the guidelines for how people in business ought to act, the morals that keep professionals conducting themselves properly and help folks resist the temptation to veer off into malpractice.

---

[1]Of course one size doesn't fit all – there are those who shun wealth, who even thrive with but very meager belongings, for their particular, individual purposes. But such individuals need not be thwarted in the slightest by those who do pursue wealth, any more than fans of baseball need to be thwarted by fans of tennis or dirt biking or Gregorian chanting.

[2]St. Thomas Aquinas, "That Man's Happiness Does not Consist in Wealth," *Summa Contra Gentiles*, Chapter xxx, in Patrick Murray, ed., *Reflections on Commercial Life* (London: Routledge, 1997), p. 89.

1.   THE FOUNDATION OF BUSINESS ETHICS

Ethics is a discipline specializing in the examination of answers to the questions "How should I act?" or "What standards ought I to use to guide my conduct?" This is not a trouble-free discipline, by any means – many prominent thinkers consider it bogus, as they might view astrology, mainly because they deny the twin supports on which ethics rests, namely, that human beings can make *bona fide* choices and that there can be some firm standard by which to judge the choices they make.[3] "Ought" implies "can," which is to say that acting on any answer to the question of ethics or any of its divisions, including business ethics, assumes that we have both the freedom to choose how we act, and certain standards for acting rightly versus wrongly.

Assuming, for now, that ethics is a *bona fide* area of human concern, business ethics is a division of professional ethics, focusing on the special areas of commerce and the profession of business. It seeks the right answer to the question *"How ought I to act, in my capacity as a commercial agent or professional merchant, manager, marketer, advertiser, executive and even consumer?"* Unlike the other major discipline that looks at business, namely economics, business ethics does not assume that there are innate motives driving one to maximize profits or utilities or long term self-interest. Business ethics, as any other look at human morality, takes it that we are all capable of doing the right or the wrong thing and that we aren't naturally driven either way – it's up to us which we will chose. That, too, is the assumption underlying criminal law in most societies.

Given the nature of ethics as such, it follows that if one's will is tyrannized, regimented, regulated, etc., in the bulk of one's life, one cannot act ethically, because then one is not making the decisions as to how one will act. To claim that a banker or employer or advertiser ought to do or avoid doing such and such, that individual must be able to choose, and there must be some way of showing that what he or she should or should not do is possible. Barring that, all talk of ethics, including business ethics, is just lamentation, as when one complains about bad or cheers good weather. This, indeed, also explains why such institutions as slavery and serfdom are widely seen to be assaults on human dignity, since they rob people of the capacity to be morally responsible agents.[4]

---

[3] For more on this see Tibor R. Machan, "A Brief Essay on Free Will," in John Burr and Milton Goldinger, eds., *Philosophy and Contemporary Issues* (Englewood Cliffs, NJ: Prentice-Hall, 2003). For a fuller discussion of business ethics itself, see Tibor R. Machan & James E. Chesher, *A Primer on Business Ethics* (Lanham, MD: Rowman & Littlefield, 2002). See, also, Ed Pols, *Acts of Our Being* (Amherst, MA: University of Massachusetts Press, 1983).

[4] To avoid misunderstanding, this doesn't mean that no one under duress has any moral responsibilities, only that with increasing duress the capacity to fulfill those responsibilities diminishes.

Liberty in human communities is secured mainly via the right to private property. If one has no authority to dispose of one's assets as one sees fit, one isn't in charge of one's own life. If others do this, by government regulation or planning, or by criminal intrusion, one cannot be responsible for one's conduct, at least to the extent one is being regimented. Paternalistic laws treat one as a child may be treated, dependent on the decisions of others and not fully responsible for how one acts.

A well-guarded right to private property is, then, a prerequisite for the exercise of virtuous conduct in any sphere but especially in commerce and business. Thus, arguably, without a substantial measure of capitalism, there cannot be any intelligible concern about business ethics, for people will lack the choice-making capacity or opportunity that is a prerequisite of ethics.

2. BUSINESS ETHICS ASSUMES THAT COMMERCE AND BUSINESS ARE, AS A RULE, MORALLY PROPER

Professions are valued human specializations: medicine, law, education, science, etc., are all professions that fulfill some good – health, justice, rearing of children, knowledge, etc.

Is there any such good that we aim for as we engage in commerce? Is there a moral virtue that requires us to strive for such a good?

Yes, the virtue of prudence, which requires us all to take reasonably good care of ourselves in life, is just such a moral virtue. The goals to be supported include prosperity, health, and knowledge. The effort to prosper, to seek to profit, is part of what the moral virtue of prudence requires from us. This assumes that our overall task is to do well at living, to flourish and succeed as rational animals here on Earth. It may be, however, that our nature is a divided one. We often assume that part of existence is otherworldly, believing that to live rightly means, in large measure, to prepare for a "life after death." And then the virtue of prudence will require not only that we conduct our lives well on Earth but also that we strive to live well in the hereafter, to the extent that we can intuit how to do so. A considerable source of consternation in human affairs stems from the attempt to balance what we require in order to live well on Earth and what we require in order to live well after death. In either case, the moral virtue of prudence requires us to be attentive to our well-being and to make an attempt to flourish.

Both commerce, for us all as amateurs, and business, as the professional extension of commerce, specialize in the production of prosperity. They are an

---

For more on this, see Tibor R. Machan, *Generosity; Virtue in Civil Society* (Washington, DC: Cato Institute, 1998).

institutionalization of certain dimensions of the moral virtue of prudence, at least vis-à-vis the requirements of flourishing on Earth or within the realm of nature, as distinct from within the realm of the supernatural.

3.   WHY, THEN, IS BUSINESS ETHICS OFTEN BUSINESS-BASHING OR BUSINESS-TAMING?

The virtue of prudence suffered a serious demotion when it was converted to the profit motive, an innate drive to promote one's self-interest. In ancient Greek philosophical ethics, as well as in other traditions of virtue ethics, prudence was seen as living carefully, doing what one's good sense or practical reason would judge to be right. But this tradition has fallen on hard times, what with the embrace by modern philosophers such as Thomas Hobbes of a mechanistic explanation of human behavior that hardly leaves room for ethics.[5]

Largely guided by the Hobbesian philosophical and methodological framework, early economists began their study by embracing the capitalist system without any kind of moral defense of it – it would have seemed odd to champion a virtue of prudence at the time, given the modern scientism[6] that prevailed among many prominent thinkers. Instead, they tended to defend capitalism for its hospitality to the innate, unavoidable human drive to seek profit. Capitalism was to be the smooth path, with minimum friction, to self-satisfaction, the sum of the achievement of which was to be the public good (also referred to as Pareto optimality or the general welfare).

Since economists, as social scientists who strive to follow the methods of the natural sciences, avoided the moral issues, critics of capitalism soon cornered the market on morality. We can see their influence throughout much of human history – if we speak of morality, we tend to think of actions that are altruistic; thus business is left off of the list of *morally* praiseworthy professions such as education, art, or science.

4.   THIS IS A MISTAKE THAT RESTS ON SEVERAL OTHERS

In fact, however, people aren't *driven* to act prudently – we have ample evidence of imprudence in human affairs which cannot be accounted for by

---

[5] For more on this, see John C. Moorehouse, "The Mechanistic Foundations of Economic Analysis," *Reason Papers*, No. 4 (1978).

[6] This is the idea that the methods and assumptions of the natural sciences ought to be implemented and embraced by all others studies, including sociology, economics, and politics. See, Tom Sorell, *Scientism: Philosophy and the Infatuation With Science* (London: Routledge, Ltd., 1991). While many natural scientists hold it, there are prominent dissenters – for example, Robert Laughlin, *A Different Universe* (New York: Basic Books, 2005).

any kind of accidental incapacitation or malfunction but is best explained by reference to human negligence. Doing what is prudent requires a choice, as well as determination or commitment, and some individuals do not make that choice. Indeed, embarking on a commercial venture is a matter of choice; the critics know this but disapprove or dispute that such a choice is a sound one.

Caring for oneself – not just about what one desires or prefers – is a prerequisite for caring for what constitutes the important elements of one's life – family, friends, community, country or humanity itself. One component of this is being economical as one lives, taking part in commerce and business wisely, diligently, and conscientiously.[7] Indeed, it means, in part, heeding the bottom line, to put it as the critics so disparagingly do.

What our commercial and business conduct needs is serious concern for doing it decently, properly. This is not a matter of bashing and taming, as if such conduct were something innately wild and vicious; rather, it involves education, especially on the producers' or sellers' side of the trade relationship. (Of course, consumers are also targeted for criticism, as when they are dismissed for their trivial pursuits, or for the "commercialization" of cultures [e.g., Christmas].)

It is a prejudice to take such a view of commerce, a prejudice that has encouraged some of the most horrible forms of human community life, including fascism, socialism (both national and international), and communism, all of which deride business and the pursuit of profit, as do some religions for obvious reasons.[8] They are false ideals and, in order for business (and indeed other aspects of earthly life) to flourish, they must be abandoned in favor of *bona fide* ethics – including of business – that teaches prudence and other virtues, such as honesty, integrity, industry, entrepreneurship and general respect for individual rights.

5.   SOME OBJECTIONS CONSIDERED

A moral philosopher could well respond to the above by asking whether, in fact, prudence is a *moral* virtue at all. Philosophically informed readers may be put in mind of Thomas Nagel's book, *The Possibility of Altruism,* which contrasts morally motivated action with prudence, defined as acting in the in-

---

[7] I propose to call this *wealth care*, to parallel what is widely taken to be the perfectly legitimate concern dubbed *health care*.

[8] Commerce tends to divert attention from the otherworldly concerns on which religions want us to focus. For more on this, see James E. Chesher and Tibor R. Machan, *The Business of Commerce, Examining on Honorable Profession* (Stanford, CA: Hoover Institution Press, 1999).

terests of one's own *future* self.[9] In the present discussion, however, a richer notion of "prudence" than Nagel's stripped-down version is being deployed.

As already hinted, 'prudence' in the modern moral philosophical era became not a virtue but an impulse, drive or instinct, following Hobbes's theory of human motivation that emerged from taking the classical physical model of how things move in nature. The drive for self-preservation or self-aggrandizement in humans is but a manifestation of the law of motion concerning momentum.

As far as its impact on moral philosophy, the Hobbesian and later social scientific account basically leaves room for a much-truncated moral life. Indeed, the idea that a person can choose to act in various ways, some (objectively) right, many quite wrong, drops out of Hobbes's deterministic picture, as it does out of that of B. F. Skinner (the 20th century behaviorist).[10]

The Hobbesian picture, with some nuances added, became the basic framework for the classical economists' idea of why people acted (behaved) as they did – they were driven to maximize utility. David Hume and Adam Smith did 'pretty up' this notion with talk of natural sympathy and such, but it remained for Immanuel Kant to revitalize a *bona fide* moral point of view, albeit at considerable cost.

In Kant, prudence retains this impulse or drive but balanced by the notion that one may be able to overcome it via the good will, which has noumenal origins – ergo Nagel's and many others' (e.g., Kurt Baier[11]) pitting of morality against prudence (with the latter's ambivalent standing).

In my understanding of business ethics, and indeed ethics as a whole, I turn to the Aristotelian virtue ethics tradition wherein prudence is practical reason, the moral virtue of choosing to be careful and to avoid wastefulness, recklessness, thoughtlessness and other forms of neglect toward one's flourishing in life.

None of this excuses corruption or charlatanism in business, any more than acknowledging the value of the health care professions excuses quackery and malpractice. What it does, however, is to identify the profession of business and commercial activities in general as being morally well-founded, decent endeavors, and those who engage in it might be called wealth-care professionals. It rescues business ethics from its frequent characterization as an oxymoron.

---

[9]Thomas Nagel, *The Possibility of Altruism* (Oxford, UK: Clarendon Press, 1970).

[10]There are others, so called soft-determinists, who make room for a peculiar version of morality. For example, there is Daniel Dennett, *Elbow Room* (Oxford, UK: Clarendon Press, 1984), who tries to construct a moral framework within the boundaries of scientific determinism, but the idea of personal responsibility for having made a wrong choice that one could have avoided making is effectively lost in this outlook.

[11]Kurt Baier, *The Moral Point of View* (New York: Random House, 1965).

6. A BRIEF ON MARKET THEORY

Before moving on to the explicitly normative topics of this work – for it is mostly about what is right and wrong or good and bad in the sphere of commerce – a few words need to be addressed to the general topic of the nature of markets, the sphere wherein commerce is conducted and wealthcare is most likely to occur. Market theories address the nature of such commerce, including its origins in human motivation, its processes, its principles of operation, and the restrictions that are sometimes erected to control those engaged in market transactions.

Markets are somewhat indistinct – for some goods and services, the entire globe is the market; for others, it may only be a small neighborhood. This is one reason that market domination is so difficult to spell out, despite the fact that that is just what would be necessary for certain public policy purposes, such as anti-trust regulations.

Markets have existed ever since people began producing goods or offering services for sale to others, even before the emergence of money, a most efficient medium of commercial exchange. However, with the demise of mercantilism – whereby government manages a region's commercial affairs – and the rise of liberal institutions, such as a substantially *laissez faire* economic policy, the significance of markets has increased enormously. So have theoretical discussions of the nature of markets, especially by economists or, before the specialty became established, political theorists. As with most social sciences, economics has been discussed from time immemorial, but until roughly the eighteenth century usually alongside such concerns as ethics, theology, politics and psychology, all tied very closely to the discipline of philosophy.

Most notable among those who advanced mature (scientific) theories of market transactions was Adam Smith (1723–1790), the Scottish moral philosopher. His work, *An inquiry into the nature and causes of the wealth of nations,* was a revolutionary analysis challenging mercantilism (the approach to economic organization practiced in modern feudal states) which concluded that in the production of most goods and services it is best to leave it to the economic agents to figure out what should be done, and to have government focus only on the legal framework within which commerce would be carried out.

Although Smith is credited with forging a social scientific approach to the study of markets, there have been economic reflections for centuries, embedded within works of ethics and political philosophy. For example, Plato (428–348 B.C.), in his famous dialogue *Republic*, sketches a theory of the division of labor but on grounds different from what later, scientific economists, advanced. Plato thought it was individual differences and not overall efficiency that justified specialization in production. Aristotle (384–322 B.C.), in his *Nicomachean Ethics* and *Politics*, also discusses economic issues, such as the

tragedy of the commons and the nature of household management. Even Dem-
ocritus of Abdera (c. 460–360 B.C.) wrote on economic topics (Gordon, 1975).

The ancients were more concerned with how economic activities fit within
the framework of living an ethical life, and organizing communities in accor-
dance with principles of justice. This way of thinking about economics and
market behavior fit within the older approach to understanding human life
in terms of whether the goals being served by agents and institutions were
worthwhile, noble, and supportive of the good human life. In the modern era,
beginning around the sixteenth century, the approach gravitated toward trying
to *explain* why men and women act the way they do, under the influence of scientism, the idea that the principles of the natural sciences are fully applicable
to the understanding of human community affairs.

Thus, following Smith's work, economics emerged as the social science
that studies markets via various theories of human motivation and behavior.
Smith himself suggested, via some pithy phrases – such as the famous "in-
visible hand" – that in markets people tend to be motivated to advance their
self-interest, although what exactly this means is still subject to debate. Some
take this to mean that we are all driven to seek to benefit ourselves first and
foremost; others, that we want to fulfill our goals, be these to our own or others' benefit; and still others, that we all want to do what *we* want to do when
we are left free to do it.

The gist of Smith's insight – very influential but not original with him (Gordon, 1975; Rothbard, 1995) – is that when not regimented by governments
or criminals, those in the marketplace will produce wealth more efficiently
than when their actions are directed for them by others (such as a government
that regulates, taxes and otherwise interferes with their commercial judgments
and conduct). Individuals in voluntary associations have a better grasp of both
what needs to be and how it can be achieved economically, and provided they
do this without force or fraud as their means, the result is most likely to be
economically – and indeed otherwise – most beneficial (which accounts for
such notions as the prudent separation of church and state, economy and state,
the arts and state, and education and state).

Over the last several centuries, commerce came to be conducted mainly
by relatively large corporations that have enjoyed, initially as grants from the
monarch and then as a matter of contract, limited liability – a protection against
severe losses from accidents or even malfeasance – making such institutions
very attractive vehicles for economic advancement and profit-making. In an
unregulated market economy, corporations are established voluntarily, not by
government as in mercantilism, so as to advance the goals of shareholders, and
business corporations serve their shareholders' economic goal of prosperity or
profit. In a mixed economy, wherein government is authorized by law to enact

laws and public policy to serve various private interests of the citizenry, businesses often lobby to gain special advantages in the market place – protection from foreign competitors, subsidies, government-backed loans, price support and so forth. This way, business corporations often act contrary to market principles by means of their political behavior.

Three ways of defending the value of markets can be distinguished: scientistic, utilitarian and rights-based.

The scientistic defense of markets rests on the philosophical legacy left by Thomas Hobbes (1588–1679), who held to the deterministic philosophy of classical mechanics (which he took from Galileo Galilei [1564–1642]) and mechanical engineering. It holds that everyone is driven to move forward, akin to the way atoms or bits of matter-in-motion do, and the less friction they encounter, the more efficient will be their forward motion. Once taken over by classical economics, this view implies that a *laissez faire* system, one with minimum governmental and criminal interference, is the most efficient for economic (and, at the hands of some economic imperialists, for all other) purposes.

The underlying idea is still the same. As Milton Friedman (1912–2006) put it, "... every individual serves his own private interest ... . The great Saints of history have served their 'private interest' just as the most money grubbing miser has served his interest. The *private interest* is whatever it is that drives an individual" (Friedman, 1976). Or, as George Stigler put it, "... Man is eternally a utility-maximizer – in his home, in his office (be it public or private), in his church, in his scientific work – in short, everywhere" (quoted in McKenzie, 1983). By this approach, economics was to have attained the status of a natural science and, for some, could generate a social engineering applied branch. That is because it would, as the natural sciences, study causes of human behavior and institutions. It would become disassociated from the methodologically more troublesome fields of ethics and political philosophy. It would not, in short, have to grapple with the problem of *values,* and could leave matters to the *causes and preferences* that motivate or drive human behavior.

The utilitarian defense – advanced by such early classical liberals as Bernard Mandeville (1670–1733), Adam Ferguson (1723–1816) and, in some of his writings, even Adam Smith – holds that if there is maximum economic liberty afoot, the greatest benefit, especially prosperity, will accrue for all. This is still a favorite normative position among many who support the free-market capitalist system. It is also referred to as the *consequentialist* case for such a system. Its early motto, forged by Mandeville, was "private vice, public benefit," meaning that even though the motivations driving market agents (ambition, greed, selfishness) may be morally objectionable, the overall outcome is laudable.

The natural rights approach to defending the market holds that all adult human beings have rights by virtue of their nature and what this requires from their community life. Advanced primarily by John Locke (1632–1704) and continued by many contemporary libertarians, the idea implies that respecting and protecting the right to private property, which is among our natural rights, makes it possible for people to pursue goals of their own choosing. These include goals motivated by the *moral virtue* of prudence, one among others we ought all to practice. Self-enhancement, including self-enrichment, is laudable in itself, even apart from any public weal which might well result from it.

Consistently respected and protected, the right to private property will also secure the optimum behavior on the part of members of a community. This is because it will require the punishment of trespassing activity, including the dumping of one's waste or failure on unwilling others. (In contrast, any system that redistributes wealth also encourages such dumping.) It is also widely accepted now that societies wherein the right to private property is part of a stable infrastructure tend to be more free, democratic and prosperous than those where no such infrastructure exists (Bethell, 1998; Pipes, 1999; Sen, 2001; Zakaria, 2003).

Of course, there are other ways that markets have been understood, explained, and defended. In recent times, the study of markets has become quite technical, deploying higher mathematics and computer science in the process. This follows a tradition in market theory established by the likes of Leon Walras (1834–1910), Vilfredo Pareto (1848–1923) and Knut Wicksell (1851–1926). Modeling markets is now a prominent approach, as are approaches that make use of evolutionary theory (Metcalfe, 1998).

Market theories are abundant, as are theories of government planning, control and regulation of economies. Certain Christian political economists – for example, Lord Acton (1834–1902), Michael Novak and Robert Sirico – argue that the necessary freedom presupposed in moral and spiritual aspiration cannot be secured without the institution of private property rights and the corresponding market system. Their primary concern with interference in market behavior doesn't focus on the obstacles such interference pose to wealth creation but on how such interference undermines freedom of choice. They note that such Christian virtues as charity and compassion are undermined by coercing people – via taxation, mainly – to "help" others or to "support" various worthy goals.

Within social scientific market theories, two stand out, namely the neoclassical and the Austrian schools. The former is perhaps the most firmly established school, with various sub-schools, including the public choice and law and economics scholars; the latter includes those who follow the teachings of Ludwig von Mises (1881–1973) and F. A. Hayek (1899–1992). Perhaps the main difference between these two schools that adhere to the idea of the market economy is that neo-classical theorists see the marketplace as an arena where individuals can satisfy their preferences by engaging in cost-benefit calculations, while the Austrian school holds that the marketplace is an arena wherein individuals discover what they want, where they form their preferences. Between the two, it is the Austrian school that tends to be more consistently and fully in support of the market approach to allocating resources in societies – e.g., Austrians tend to favor decoupling the state, from the creation and management of money (via the theory of free banking). It is also within the Austrian school that entrepreneurship, a vital element of market theory, finds its most comfortable theoretical home (Kirzner, 1973).

The criticisms of market theories are many, and only a few can be mentioned here. Among those who believe that, contrary to the social scientific economists, science supports socialism, even communism, Karl Marx (1818–1883) is, of course, the most prominent. He held that capitalism is but a stage in humanity's march toward communism, the most mature stage of its development. Marx asserted that this capitalist phase is required in much the same way an individual needs to pass through adolescence. It is a period of senseless productivity, anarchic and irrational, but useful, ultimately, because it develops tools of production which, in the subsequent socialist and communist phases, will be put to rational collective purpose. The process of which this capitalist phase is a part is inevitable, determined by laws of development, albeit not mechanical but (softly) dialectical. Humanity's development is, thus, akin to that of individual human beings, with tribalism its infancy, feudalism its childhood, capitalism its adolescence, socialism its young adulthood and communism its maturity. Marx chided Smith and Ricardo for mistaking a phase for a permanent condition, and rejected the idea that markets are universal phenomena in human community affairs.

Market theory is also criticized by such interventionists as John Maynard Keynes (1883–1946), who believed that, while basically productive, the system is ultimately both unjust and subject to upheavals that can only be avoided through government action. Keynes held, in *The End of Laissez-Faire* (1927), that the market left the poor and weak behind, thus accommodating crude Social Darwinism and injustice. And he also thought that fully free markets are subject to severe business cycles that require moderation by demand-side government interference such as public works projects and related expenditures and, of course, the corresponding tax policies.

From political theory proper, the free market has been criticized on many grounds, including, most prominently, that it tends to reward luck rather than effort, by making it possible for consumers to spend their resources on what they like – e.g., the beauty or talents of lucky people – rather than on what is just and proper – safety and security in life. Rawls, who was the main proponent of this position in the 20th century, advocated such a system of justice

as fairness, wherein the harshness of capitalism would be offset by principles of egalitarianism, generating a welfare state or mixed system. Inequality
would only be acceptable where it advanced the lot of the worst-off in society –
for example, when someone's inventiveness or creativity is disproportionately
compensated because the person helps so many of the poor.

Another criticism of capitalist free-market theory is that it is too individualistic – atomistic – and ignores the fundamentally social aspect of human
nature. Charles Taylor, among philosophers, and Amitai Etzioni, among the
more popular intellectuals, champion communitarianism, wherein the consistent and strict individual-rights approach, including vis-à-vis private property,
is rejected in favor of community governance. Such governance would benefit
the community as a whole, even if individuals were unwilling to accept this
benefit on their own. (Etzioni has used the example of random drugs searches,
which he believes can benefit the community but which would be resisted by
innocent as well as guilty citizens, and could be so resisted in a regime of strict
property rights.) As Taylor argues, one *belongs* to the community, and one's
self is actually part of a network of selves, not something individual, unique.
Markets do not always manage to accommodate such a communitarian conception of human nature and community life.

In answer to the Marxists, market theorists insist that, at a most fundamental level, human nature remains stable over time, despite technological and
related changes, so some principles of community life, including the basics of
economic relationships, persist, and these reflect the market theory approach,
not the historicist view championed by Marx.

As far as Keynes was concerned, the gist of the market theory reply is that
he placed mysterious confidence in government's ability to deal with what he
took to be market failures (which, in any case, resulted from earlier government intervention – e.g., the Great Depression, which was brought on by the
federal banks' bad monetary policy). Even if there are market failures, political remedies run even greater risks – as developed by the public choice
theorists James M. Buchanan and Gordon Tullock, for example. For example,
governments might establish monopolies in the delivery of "public" utilities
to prevent duplication of equipment, only to find that strikes could cripple the
industry, something that could only be avoided by prohibiting strikes, which is
itself a considerable political failure.

Turning, finally, to communitarianism, the market theorist concedes that
human nature has a crucial social element to it, but refuses to admit that this
overrides the crucial individualist aspect of every human being, namely, the
need to make choices and decisions, even about whether to belong to one or
another community. This distinctive element of human nature, that adult men
and women are responsible for directing their own lives, even in regard to

social relationships, is best accommodated in a system of laws in which the institution of private property is central.

Various hybrids have also been proposed between the market and the centrally or democratically planned systems, especially since the demise of Soviet-style socialism. For example, market socialism, economic democracy and the welfare state all enjoy support from those who are not convinced that the free market is adequate for human economic life. Market socialists wish to retain socialism at the political level but leave many segments of society to the laws of the market place. Economic democrats reject centrally planned socialist aspirations but believe that the political process of democracy should also be applied to society's economic affairs. The welfare state is gaining support from those who admit that markets provide superior performance in productivity, innovation, and entrepreneurship, but insist that without welfare legislation they would leave too many in society in dire straits.

As with any theory about human community life, the likelihood of the actualization of a fully free-market system is quite problematic. Even if market theory, in general, shows that the free market is the most cogent way of understanding and guiding human economic affairs, it is unlikely that men and women in even the most enlightened communities will steadfastly embrace and implement it. (This can be appreciated even if one holds to some competing theory, since any theory, however sound, faces the challenge of human diversity and even stubbornness.)

Ultimately, the three types of defenses of free markets each make a valid point: (1) an unregulated market economy is routinely more efficient for purposes of economically enriching the community of which it is a part; (2) it is also one in which the efforts of individuals to promote their own goals and purposes tend to lead to maximum overall welfare; and, finally, (3) free markets best accommodate the need of every adult individual to live virtuously, responsibly, and prudently (without holding out the impossible, utopian promise of a system that will make everyone happy). The ethical life is impossible when others are in charge of the ethical agent, and in free markets this is prohibited.

A final issue which may be useful to discuss is why economics became a social science in the first place and whether there could be a resurgence of normative economic analysis. One difficulty with normative economics is that it would accept the idea that aspiring to riches or prosperity is a worthwhile human endeavor. Yet this was in considerable dispute throughout history – e.g., in Christianity it is doubtful that such aspirations are morally noteworthy. In the main, most moral theories demean wealth-seeking, while economics studies wealth-seeking and its innumerable permutations. One way to avoid flying in the face of the prevailing moral scorn of wealth-seeking is to identify the motivation to seek wealth as instinctive – we are driven or hardwired to do this. There can be no moral complaint about the study of something that is innately tied to our behavior and institutions; by contrast, if seeking wealth is a matter of free will, it may have to be accepted as something insidious.

The dilemma is clear: either economics is normative, in which case those who consider it sound must strive to establish its moral legitimacy; or economics is descriptive (as most academic economists would have it), in which case one of the most important aspects of market behavior, namely, free economic and commercial choices by its participants, ultimately is left ethically unfounded. The discipline will continue to grapple with this problem, but it isn't alone in facing the dilemma. Such fields as ecology and environmental studies, not to mention psychology, psychiatry, sociology, and political science also confront the problem of whether to view human behavior in the tradition of deterministic science – admittedly dealing with a very complex entity – or to make room for the moral viewpoint, with its presupposition that human beings can make choices and take the initiative (and thus, for example, can be culpable for mismanaging the environment [Schwartz & Begley, 2002]).

Indeed, this is a problem that faces any culture wherein science is prominent and has lead to many momentous and mostly welcome results. Must this mean the dehumanization and demoralization of such a culture? Some kind of successful rapprochement is needed so as to secure a happy coexistence between science, technology and the moral perspective on human life (McCloskey, 1985).

7.   ON PRIVATE PROPERTY RIGHTS

These reflections on aspects of a commercial society should conclude with a discussion of the most fundamental prerequisite for business, namely, the legal recognition of the right to private property. It is a widely misunderstood principle, to say the least, often by the very folks who stand by it most vociferously.

That misguided understanding of the right to private property – and of the free market spawned by it – has to do with what George Hotchkiss of NYU said many moons ago, namely, "People are primarily interested in themselves and the things that pertain to them – their homes, their children, their health, complexion, comfort, recreation, financial security, their friends, their own struggles and triumphs of daily life."[12] While there is some truth in this, there is also much that the statement neglects.

For one, sadly, too many people are not diligently enough interested in themselves – certainly not in taking good care of themselves, their children, etc. Too often they are quite negligent, which makes it plausible to promote the idea that they need to be cared for by others, even in their adulthood.

---

[12]George Hotchkiss, *An Outline of Advertising* (New York, The Macmillan Company, 1933).

More importantly here, however, many people, while taking reasonable care of themselves, are also very interested in promoting various causes that do not directly involve them at all. They want to contribute to the arts, to curing various diseases, to advancing the sciences, and to advocating certain political ideas, ideals or public policies. Indeed, billions and billions of dollars are spent on such goals that do not directly benefit the persons themselves who do the giving (except in the amorphous sense that they are interested in these goals).

If it is clearly understood that the respect and protection of the right to private property facilitates not only the pursuit of one's direct, immediate self-interest but also all those other projects that people so evidently and widely support, then the abrogation of that right can be seen in a different light from the usual.

Many who oppose private property rights do so on the grounds that they hold to the Hotchkiss position – it simply facilitates the pursuit of private goals. Thus it must neglect others and impersonal goals. But if we understand that private property rights facilitate much else besides taking good care of one's immediate concerns, including many of the concerns I have listed above, then attacking it takes on a very different coloration.

Attacking private property rights comes down not so much to making sure that people don't just care for themselves as to making sure that they don't get to choose what the goals are that gain support, including goals having little to do with themselves. In other words, attacking private property rights amounts to attacking the right of individuals to decide what kind of goals they get to support and how much support these goals receive.

Putting it a bit differently, attacking the right to private property amounts to attacking the judgments of private individuals who would have the option to support various goals they believe in. Instead, government officials – politicians, bureaucrats and their advisors – get to confiscate private property in the form of taxes and other takings, and they get to say to what ends these will be contributed.

But seeing it this way should make us all realize that the issue isn't about "selfish versus benevolent" goals but about who gets to be benevolent and who gets to say who and what will be benefited. Why, one might ask, should it be people with political clout who get to make that decision? Are they really better at making such decisions? Are they really less likely to engage in unreasonable acquisitiveness, to be greedy, to be narrow-minded, and/or to serve vested interests?

In fact, the evidence seems clear that those in politics are far more inclined to serve vested interests than are ordinary folks who, on their own, tend to be quite generous. Billions of dollars, for example, are sent abroad by American citizens, all on their own initiative, to help people who are in dire straits, and more still is contributed to various domestic causes.

Besides, the idea that those going into politics or becoming bureaucrats are the most benevolent types in society is, despite what they often wish to have us believe, so contrary to what we all know from the daily news, not to mention serious scholarship,[13] as to be utterly ridiculous. It is sheer gullibility to believe such a thing, but because of this mistaken notion regarding the right to private property and some defenses of it, it gains undeserved credibility. It's time to recognize the confusion – or indeed trick – for what it is, namely, a way to bamboozle people into relinquishing their right to distribute their own resources as they judge best when they are, indeed, the ones in the best position to judge.

---

[13]This, of course, is the substance of *public choice theory*, advanced in James M. Buchanan and Gordon Tullock, *The Calculus of Consent* (University of Michigan Press, 1962), for which Buchanan received the Nobel Prize in 1985.

Chapter 2

OWNERSHIP RIGHTS AND COMMERCE

1. IS COMMERCE DECENT?

Let us begin with the most important question about business, the profession that cares about wealth and that has as its goal its enhancement. Business arises as the professional arm of commerce. We all engage in commerce but not all of us work in business. This is not unlike medicine: we all dabble in self-medication but few of us are doctors, nurses and such. Those are the professionals in that sphere.

We need to ask, first of all, whether embarking on wealthcare is all right from the moral point of view. Is business itself a decent profession?

Some might consider this an odd question but, given that business is held in low esteem by many cultural commentators, as well as by Hollywood, pulp fiction writers like John Grisham, and dramatists like the late Arthur Miller (whose *Death of a Salesman* depicts business as a pathetic, lowly profession) or David Mamet (whose *Glengarry Glen Ross* characterizes people in business as most conniving), the question is not at all negligible. Charles Baudelaire, the famed French poet, said that "The spirit of every business-man is completely depraved. ... Commerce is satanic, because it is the basest and vilest form of egoism."[14]

Should we accept this condemnation of a field of work – and its practitioners – that has managed to create prosperity and wealth for not only those who succeed in it but those who are indirect beneficiaries of its products, such as universities, museums, and think tanks?

Most people take it for granted that medicine, education, and science have merit, and that individuals doing work in those fields are doing something worthwhile. They can claim credit for having chosen a fine calling or vocation. But the same is not so with business. A clear indication of this is that there is a great deal of talk about the social responsibility of corporations, and how companies should "give back to the community" by way of contributions or philanthropy, something few other professionals hear of. Are college professors being implored to do likewise? No, because their work is deemed to be worthwhile in and of itself. And why is it necessary for people in business

---

[14]Charles Baudelaire, *Intimate Journals*, trans. Christopher Isherwood (San Francisco: City Lights Books, 1983), p. 89.

to "give back"? Have they committed theft, and so need to atone for it by returning the goods they stole? No, there is something else behind the hostility toward business.

Throughout human history, in the East as well as the West, commerce has been demeaned. Plato depicted the trader as a lowly sort, in his most famous dialogue, the *Republic*. Of all types of sinners who gathered in the temple, Jesus picked on the money lenders, and the Prince of Peace violently attacked them, sending a signal that Christianity seems to have embraced throughout its history. The idea that money may be lent for interest is still attacked by some moral philosophers, as if foregoing the benefits of liquid assets does not deserve to be compensated.

Is this all okay? Should we be ashamed when we embark upon a career in business? Is it a lowly profession akin, say, to prostitution or being a prison guard at a concentration camp?

If the answer is 'no,' as I believe it is, why have so many prominent figures shown utter contempt for commerce and its professional arm, business? What accounts for this?

A good place to begin is with Aristotle, the ancient Greek philosopher, a man who had little respect for activities aimed at prosperity. He believed that the highest form of human life is that which is devoted to contemplation. He held that theorist who contemplate the eternal verities are doing the most honorable thing, and this idea is still with us. Professors and educators in general are usually held in high esteem (unless they become popular and make money!). The Nobel Prize is usually given to theoreticians, not to those who put theories into practice. The bad guys in novels, movies and television are usually the ones trying to make a profit.

One problem with Aristotle's ethics is that he believed that what is exclusively important in our lives is that we have minds. To be good, for him, meant being exclusively focused on what the mind uses, namely ideas. Intellectuals, then, seem to live the most, if not the only, worthy lives.

This is not really true, however. We are not just mental beings – we are embodied. And we need to be good at applying our thinking to all facets of our being, not just to abstract ideas. We need to succeed as living, thinking, biological entities, not only as intellectuals. (Of course, there is much debate on just what Aristotle meant. But what we might call "intellectualism" has been the most influential aspect of his ethical reflections.)

Oddly enough, it is one of the main virtues Aristotle himself identified, namely prudence, that gives commerce and business its clear link with morality or ethics. To be frugal, industrious, and heedful of the bottom line is something demanded by prudence, provided we view ourselves not simply as mental but as biological (albeit thinking) entities.

Such an understanding of human life shows that professionals in business are carrying out important tasks, every bit as much as professionals in medicine, science, education or engineering. It does not mean, of course, that such professionals cannot fall prey to the temptation of corruption. But this is no less true in education, science or any other profession. There are quacks in medicine, frauds in science, and so on, just as there are cheats in business. As a profession, however, business isn't like prostitution, pimping or drug pushing, undertakings that are inherently morally questionable.

Why is all this of significance? Especially after September 11, 2001, when terrorism was directed at both the major substance and the greatest symbol of commerce, the World Trade Center, it should be evident that whether business is a good thing is disputed even today, despite the evident beneficial nature of the institution. Not everyone acknowledges what is evident or reasonable. Moreover, many who embark upon business, professionally or otherwise, haven't the faintest notion of what makes this profession worthwhile. They engage in it absentmindedly and, when challenged, do not know what makes it honorable. There are even people in business who look upon what they do with self-deprecation and cynicism. They see themselves as so-called practical people who have abandoned naïve idealism and thus can pursue business because they do not care whether it is immoral, amoral or moral.

Certainly such people aren't going to make convincing defenders of this very large element of Western culture. And yet the institution does require a defense, given the bad press it has gotten throughout history and continues to get from many circles – philosophical, theological, ethical and cultural.

Furthermore, when professionals turn cynical about what they do, they aren't going to be inclined to worry much about doing it properly and ethically. So, in consequence, business practices can suffer. The usual approach is to say that all that matters is whether the law is obeyed, regardless of ethics and decency.

The law, however, is not a sufficient guide to proper business conduct because it changes from country to country, even from state to state. Unless those in business are guided by certain sound principles of business ethics, they will eventually lose their way. It is sometimes held that philosophy and its various branches are for people who are lost in the clouds, absentminded people, but there is a good case that contradicts that view. Without some understanding of the philosophical underpinnings of both the criticism and the defense of business, the profession will always suffer from moral ambiguity, and that means it is going to be unstable and morally suspect.

None of this means that all people in business need to become well versed in the field of intellectual history. But they do need to be aware that sometimes they may have to dip into that field to consult those who have contributed to the on-going dialogue about the merits of trade, commerce, finance, capitalism, market processes and so forth. They need to be aware that there is such a conversation going on, and that it has strong implications for the way business is understood and depicted throughout the world. It may even have an impact on how people in business are treated, whether respected or held in contempt, something that, as we know, can have a powerful impact on the lives of those professionals.

There is a lot of discussion afoot about the origins of the Holocaust, but it is not mentioned often enough that one thing that contributed to it was the hatred of business. Jews, unlike Christians, did not have any religious objections to trade and finance; quite the contrary. When they settled in Christian countries, they were usually the ones who took up commercial trades. Often, this gave them considerable clout, for which they were then envied, resented, even despised. This is not a negligible portion of the story of one of human history's worst events. (And it is also important to realize that, despite being Jewish himself, Karl Marx considered the Jews to be open to severe criticism on the grounds that they were the quintessential capitalists, traders! This is not all that far from why the Nazis found Jews objectionable.)

People in business, like those in engineering and medicine, work in a field that unabashedly champions life here on Earth. Still, their work is not always well received; in fact, it is often demeaned. For capitalism, free markets and commerce in general to gain moral standing, this needs to be rejected, and the reasons why the critics are misguided need to be understood – even by those in business, at times! A good beginning might be to explore the implications of another observation made by Charles Baudelaire, namely that "Commerce is natural, therefore shameful." What if someone said this about medicine or science in general? Think about it!

2.   COMMERCE IS HUMANIZING

Sure, you say, what's with this idea – doesn't everyone know it already? Well, actually, in many academic institutions, you will find professors of this and that proclaiming just the opposite. They claim commerce is a dehumanizing institution that makes people treat one another as objects or, at most, as means to various ends, not as full persons.

The doctrine is called "commodification" – making people into commodities, things for nothing other than to be purchased. The charge is that in a fully capitalist, free-market society, the system would encourage everyone to treat all others as mere useful products, like one's chair or automotive tires. For this reason, the argument goes – and it got its biggest boost from Karl Marx, in the 19th Century when he took capitalism to task very influentially for doing all kinds of nasty things to people – the free market, with its capitalist economic system, is not really good for human beings at all.

At first sight, this may sound like a credible point to make against capitalism. When you go to the grocery store, for example, you tend to treat the cashier or the manager as no more than a means to your ends of walking out of the place with what you need at home. You don't much socialize with these people, at least not initially. They are just functionaries to you. If they were machines and could do what you needed from them, that would be perfectly fine. Or so it can seem, from a superficial examination of what happens in markets. Your broker, doctor, auto mechanic, shoe repairer and the rest aren't your personal friends. They are instruments used to satisfy important needs of yours, but they could easily be replaced with someone else or with some tool. (Nowadays, you can even check out by using auto-scanners, with no need for a person at all.)

The trouble is that to focus on this element of the market – that it is mostly impersonal on a certain level – betrays a narrow vision. As if people would leave it at that, except in the most unusual circumstances – for example, when they are in a hurry and need to get done with shopping as quickly as possible. But normally that isn't how it is, at all.

As my friend and fellow philosophy professor Neera K. Badhwar argued in a well-developed, complex paper on the topic, commerce is actually the institution where much of our intimate social life gets its start. And anyone can check this out easily enough.[15]

Just consider that, wherever you work, you have colleagues with whom you have perfectly human relationships, good or bad or in between. In fact, sometimes places of work nearly become homes away from home, where people not only meet and talk and grow close (to enjoy or be annoyed by each other), but get involved quite seriously in each other's lives. Kids are discussed, as are spouses. Close friendships, or at least palships, develop frequently. Some colleagues become lovers, even marry in time. (Contrast this with how it is likely to go at the DMV!)

The myth that market transactions are impersonal is just that, a myth, and it comes from shallow, superficial reflection on what goes on in markets. It may be no accident that the idea is so popular in the academy, where there is often a kind of isolation among faculty, with few becoming close with one another, although there are enough exceptions to this that it should raise doubts in the minds of those who spread the myth about the market.

Even down at the grocery store – or the pet shop or car dealer – customers and vendors frequently depart from their initial reason for coming together, and start talking about sports, ethnic food, music or family troubles. And from that, now and then, full-blown, genuine friendships emerge.

---

[15]Neera K. Badhwar, "Friendship and Commercial Societies," in Bernard Schumacher, ed. *L'amitie* (Paris: Presses Universitaires de France, 2005).

What the critics don't appreciate is how well people can multitask in life, that while they do business they can also do arts, sciences, education, family affairs and the rest, on the side. Karl Marx was wrong – the free market is by no means only a cash nexus, where everyone thinks only of the bottom line. It would be entirely unnatural for human beings to be that way.

3.   CALCULATION PROBLEM & TRAGEDY OF THE COMMONS

I wish here to take note of two interesting aspects of economics. I want to explain them clearly so that anyone will be able to see their point and how they are actually related.

In a nutshell, the famous calculation problem facing centrally planned economies (identified by Ludwig von Mises and his followers) and the famous tragedy of the commons (hinted at, early on, by Thucydides and Aristotle, and developed more fully by Garret Hardin) are, in effect, two sides of the same coin. One side is the description, while the other is the evaluation of the same phenomenon, namely, the refusal to recognize private property rights in human affairs.

Put briefly, here is the calculation problem: when individuals are not owners of resources, they are not able to assess their value, and when resources are publicly owned, their use will be systematically hasty and imprudent. As the 1975 Nobel Laureate F. A. Hayek explained it:

> ... It is more than a metaphor to describe the price system of telecommunications which enables individual producers to watch merely the movements of a few pointers, as an engineer might watch the hands of a few dials, in order to adjust their activities to changes of which they may never know more than is reflected in the price movement.[16]

Hayek's point is that, when one owns resources, one allocates just the amount of it to this or that purchase, based on what one knows of one's own circumstances, needs, wants, etc., which, in turn, contributes to an overall telecommunications system that serves to inform consumers and producers, and thus manages the allocation of resources throughout the market place.

As to the tragedy of the commons, here is how Thucydides explained it, many moons ago:

> [T]hey devote a very small fraction of the time to the consideration of any public object, most of it to the prosecution of their own objects. Meanwhile, each fancies that no harm will come to his neglect, that it is the business of somebody else to

---

[16]F. A. Hayek, *Individualism & Economic Order* (London: Routledge & Kegan Paul, 1948), pp. 86–7.

> look after this or that for him; and so, by the same notion being entertained by all separately, the common cause imperceptibly decays.[17]

Here, the idea is that, when resources are owned commonly and all have access to their use, they will be depleted much faster than under a system of private ownership. Nor will they likely be replaced, under such common ownership.

Of course, that individuals are not able to assess the value of things to them may or may not be a good thing. Only if they ought to be able to do so could this be something bad. But when we realize that public ownership leads to systematic haste and imprudence – for example, because resources are quickly depleted if no one knows the limits of use to which these resources may be put – then we get a hint that the inability of assessing the value of resources has deleterious consequences for most of us, though with no one to blame for this except, perhaps, those who insist on keeping the institution of public ownership in force.

That's the tragedy. No one is in a position to assess just how much of the resources contained in the commons available for us is available to any particular one of us, so as much as can be accessed and used will, in fact, be consumed. This will involve taking as much (and as quickly) as possible, while others scramble equally hard to do the same. The resulting depletion is not, then, a matter of greed or something else unreasonable but of doing the most that can be done so as to achieve one's very likely legitimate goals.

It is an underlying assumption of both the tragedy and the calculation problem that individual human beings, not collectives, tribes or communities, make decisions concerning how resources will be used. Indeed, in an absolute monarchy, where the king owns everything and no one else has the recognized authority to decide on the disposition and use of anything, there is no tragedy of the commons, or any kind of calculation problem. The country is deemed to be one huge piece of private property; whatever the king decides is exactly the efficient thing to do, and however resources are allocated is precisely the best way to allocate them. Those who must go without do not matter, since it is the king's decision that they should go without. And the materials that get depleted are exactly what ought to be depleted, given that this king has so decreed.

Of course, since the king isn't really the only person with the rightful authority to make decisions about everything, this system isn't going to succeed very long. The king will be resisted, on and off, and eventually deposed by someone who promises better recognition of the sovereignty of members of the society.

Let's explore the tragedy of the commons in concrete terms. Consider that a cattle rancher is interested in supplying his cattle with as much feed as he

---

[17]Thucydides, *The History of the Peloponnesian War*, bk. I, sec. 141.

can. It is not a matter of what one owns or has obtained via rental, but of the effectiveness of the scramble. All the ranchers are under the impression that the commons is available to them, so they will all try as hard as possible to obtain as much as they can, and this will lead to a kind of grabbing from the commons before others take what they want. This can occur in the case of ranchers using common grazing fields, or special interest groups and their lobbyists taking as much as they are able to take via the political process of voting and related means for getting something from the treasury.

When it comes to commonly owned resources, such as public lakes, rivers, the atmosphere, or forests, this process leads to conduct that is often considered greedy, but which merely consists of supplying oneself with what one believes one may be able to make good use of, for purposes of pursuing one's goals. Painters, scholars, scientists, merchants, and all will follow this policy of taking the resources and running away with them, not because they are evil or wicked but because they are committed to their tasks.

The way in which this resembles the calculation problem is not all that difficult to understand. Without private ownership of the resources, the value of such resources is indeterminable. Private owners look to other private owners, and those who purchase them, to establish the prices of resources. Differential utilization of the resources will prompt different people to ask for and pay different prices, leading to a helpful if not flawless communication system concerning how important the resources are, in a given market place. But the commons do not permit such determination and, as a result, impedes communication between users and suppliers.

One might think, as did socialist planners, that some central authority, standing in for the public (as seen by a dictator or democratic assembly), could tell just how much of the resources should be used by whom, and for what purpose. But no general purpose exists to which such a determination can be made to conform (other than in small groups, perhaps, such as a family, kibbutz, convent, or commune wherein the few members come to agree on their common goals).

So the depletion of resources is necessarily unguided by coordination of supply and demand throughout the market via the more or less accurate registration of individual or small-group wants and needs. In this way, then, the tragedy of the commons and the calculation problem amount to two distinct but related facets of the same obstacle to central planning or even mere government regulation. What they have firmly in common is that they arise from the vital fact of human individuality, a central feature of human life that only the free marketplace can accommodate optimally.

4. ATTACK BY DISTORTION – THE LOWDOWN ON GLOBALIZATION

Suppose someone described the game of golf by reference to riding in carts, wearing funny pants and large shirts, and occasionally using the various clubs to beat one's dog. Would this be fair? Someone who gave such a definition of the game would probably be on a warpath to disparage it, not to explain its true nature.

Consider, then, how the critics of globalization deal with that far more important contemporary phenomenon, globalization (which, by the way, isn't all that contemporary since, in certain periods of the modern era, globalization was in full advance). These critics point to the fact that globalization is sometimes related to child labor; it can involve various strains for insidious nationalism, such as trying to whip a country's economy into shape by coercion; and it can also involve some regional collusion (as with the European Union). Indeed, when so characterized – or should we say caricatured – globalization looks like an evil unleashed upon the globe by demons, instead of a promising method to promote economic prosperity and political liberty, fostered by sensible political economists (beginning with Adam Smith himself).

Why would some folks hate globalization as it is properly conceived? Why would they be so eager to distort its nature and paint it in a bad light?

We could ask the same thing about those who would distort the nature of golf, or marriage, or education. Enemies of golf might think that there is too much money spent on the sport, at the expense of their own favorite pastime. Enemies of marriage might wish to discredit it because they have failed at it royally and now wish to make free love or some other kind of union respectable. Enemies of education might want to have folks believe that all there is to it is indoctrination in dogmas the old wish for the young to accept uncritically, since they themselves don't much like to learn and find intellectual effort unpleasant.

So what might be some reasons for disliking *bona fide* globalization so much that it is then mischaracterized to make it seem a menace?

For one, the removal of international trade barriers, the central theme of globalization, unleashes competition which is the nemesis of entrenched industries and labor groups. It is sort of like the famous American "dream team" that was sent to the Barcelona Olympics – they were completely unbeatable for a time, but eventually other countries started to learn and catch up, and the dream team could not continue to win without improving its own game, without doing hard work to stay on top.

Industry, including labor, often would like nothing better than to achieve prominence in the market and then stay there effortlessly. There is much of this tendency everywhere – including academic life, where many people wish to coast regarding their discipline without keeping up, without doing anything past when they received tenure. When young Turks turn up, as it were, and challenge the old guard, this is not often received with welcome. In principle, academics, like others, are supposed to keep improving and invite challenge and criticism from their colleagues, but there is corruption there, as there is elsewhere, and it often results in barrier to entry – refusing tenure to a challenging young teacher or scholar, or their equivalent.

This is one of the several reason globalization is resisted – the motive is known as protecting one's vested interest – and members of many industries (for example, farming) evince it aplenty.

Another reason is the widespread belief that if we open up markets and encourage international commerce, this will eliminate or diminish national and cultural distinctiveness. And there is something to this, though not much. It does not take a genius to see that the marketplace unites people on some levels, but by no means on all – just go to any mall and see the enormous diversity of shoppers and merchants. The bulk of them accept the common medium of exchange and the ethics of commerce that should guide everyone, without any threat whatsoever to personal, cultural, religious identity.

Of course, there are some groups wherein such a practice conflicts with principles of free trade: If your tribe enslaves certain people, this will certainly be threatened by globalization, since slaves experience the harshest barriers of all to free trade. If the dominant male citizens in some country treat women badly and wish to bar them from economic power, this, too, is going to be threatened by freedom of trade.

One of the main enemies of globalization is the widespread belief that living a good life is itself something of an affront! People should suffer here on Earth, not enjoy their lives, and globalization promises many folks just the opposite, namely, prosperous living.

Under the guise of globalization, some dirty practices are also possible, of course, and some people mistake this for consequences of the real thing. For example, taking your firm abroad because in the host country you can dump your soot into the atmosphere with impunity may appear to be consistent with freedom of trade, but it isn't. To raise the question as to who has the basic right, the person to breathe clean air or the person to dump soot into the air, is a bit like raising the question of who has the basic right, the person to go around uninjured by a gunshot wound or the person who wants to shoot that person. Dumping soot into the air-mass that is inevitably going to land in the lungs of non-consenting people is a violation of their rights. That should be a crime, because people are being assaulted and freedom of trade cannot tolerate such an assault among trading partners. Globalization, in fact, should encourage the enactment of laws that protect life and property from assault, including pollution.

There is a problem with attempting to provide a collectivist type of cost-benefit analysis of globalization, including the creation of pollution of public spheres, because such analysis fails to consider individual rights and objectives. It assumes some standard that at least most people want followed but fails to consider what quite a few others may aim for – for example, those who are not risk-averse or who aren't so sensitive to pollutants.

When it comes to how the system would work out, I suggest we do not listen to those who are hostile to globalization in any form, any more than we should ask those who disparage golf or marriage about the nature of those pursuits.

There is also the idea, already noted, that anyone who thinks globalization is some novel phenomenon in the world is misinformed. One need only consider the Olympic Games, in both ancient and modern times, to realize how wrong is that idea.

The Olympic Games include nearly all the countries in the world, and competitors from all of the member-countries can take part in the many events. And, yes, they all abide by the same rules.

If that isn't globalization, then I don't know what is.

When we consider economic globalization, it's about how all the people around the globe need to play by the same economic rules – free trade. No one gets to enslave workers – they must be hired and bargained with. No one gets to violate contracts – they must be honored and if not, the law steps in to rectify any breaches that have occurred. No one gets to deprive another of his or her property – only voluntary exchanges are kosher. And so it goes, into the minute details of commerce.

Critics of globalization complain that such general principles of commerce may not suit everyone, so let's not attempt to make them ubiquitous as globalization would have them be. Why? Because of cultural differences that should not be destroyed.

Has the Olympics destroyed cultural differences? No. Of course, in some areas there has been increased uniformity, but by no means in all. The costumes the athletes wear, and the music they prefer, say, in performances skating or synchronized swimming, will be different, and I am sure they also eat different foods and speak their own languages when communicating with others from their countries.

This only proves that human beings across the globe can share many practices and still keep their own special, even unique, ways, with no conflict at all. Just as the comic actor and novelist Steve Martin puts it in his most recent novella, *The Pleasure of My Company* (Hyperion Books, 2003), "People, I thought. These are people. Their general uniformity was interrupted only by their individual variety." And this is true not just of individual but also of innumerable group varieties. Both the attempt to make us all the same – the great fault of communism and other totalitarian ideologies – and the attempt to keep us all different – which is what some of the modern subjectivist and deconstructionist schools promote – are off-base.

Just think – most people around the globe communicate in language, write and speak it, yet these are different languages. They live in homes, yet their architecture varies enormously. The majority get dressed every day, but certainly their styles of dress are highly diverse. Cuisine, artistic styles, forms of dance – you name it, and it is both universal and incredibly varied.

Globalization, too, involves some practices that everyone would have to follow, without in the slightest depriving people of their individuality, cultural variety, personality types and so forth. All this is quite natural, and there is no need at all for various lobby groups to butt in to make it work out their way. In addition, as stressed so nicely in Tyler Cowan's book, *Creative Destruction* (Princeton University Press, 2004), there is so much interplay between these different styles that new ones come every day, while old ones disappear, all quite naturally.

Of course, the fact that people wish to control how these matters proceed is also a fact of life, but it is not the same kind of difference as those mentioned above. In the cases of diverse styles of dance, art, language and such, most came about spontaneously, without some dictator ordering how things should go. But when governments introduce protectionist measures, subsidies, price-support programs and other restraints of trade, that's different. Here we see the central uncivil element in human relations, the introduction of coercion, of some people dictating how others must behave. It's a difference that is insidious, hostile to human nature, not part of the natural pluralism of human life.

So what needs to be excluded from human affairs, the only thing the law should really worry about everywhere, is the way that some people try to take over the lives of others by compelling them to do as they would have them do. The rest will work out pretty well, with only the ordinary human failings upsetting matters, and few of those can go very far without the individuals or groups perpetrating them having power over others.

5.   GLOBALIZATION'S AGGRAVATIONS

What many people object to in globalization is not all that different from what they object to in capitalism – free markets are highly volatile; jobs can be found and then lost; products appear and then disappear; services cost too little and then too much; innovations displace products we have gotten used to but we also benefit from them, big time; commerce seems to take over culture, eradicate distinctions, etc. There is what Joseph Schumpeter called "creative destruction" going on all the time and when its impact is felt by oneself or one's loved ones, it is not always welcome.

Yet, the benefits of globalization, as of capitalism, are mostly accepted without much hesitation. Less expensive clothing, cars, electronics, travel, and so forth are rarely lamented. And the great variety of goods and services and all that this makes possible is also widely welcome.

One thing that underlies the complaints about globalization and capitalism is that these upset the status quo. Just after one has moved into a neighborhood, settled into a new home and placed one's kids into schools, joined a church, all of this can be turned upside down by an economic transition – the firm one works for is downsizing, is moving abroad, is outsourcing one's work, or something else akin to these. Not that this happens a lot but it can and that is scary to most folks.

Yet, at the same time, few people really prefer stagnation. When computers replaced typewriters, few protested. When CDs replaced cassettes, again there was but the faintest protest, mostly from those involved in manufacturing the obsolete product. And this has been going on for generations – the consuming public welcomes innovation, improvements on products and services that come from the encouraging conditions of free markets, while in some industries there is panic.

So, unions are notorious for promoting featherbedding, making jobs that have no real function any longer. A most recent case reported involved a new urinal that doesn't require flushing. Don't ask me for the details – it's a baffling idea. But, the story goes, when in Philadelphia it was recently introduced, the plumber's union negotiated a deal whereby despite the fact that it wasn't needed, plumbing was supplied so that plumbers wouldn't have to find new employment. This kind of thing used to be routine with the railroads, when locomotives were upgraded and unions secured deals whereby the same number of people would continue to man the engines.

Then there are the less clearly economic concerns about globalization and capitalism, having to do with feelings of nationalism, patriotism, ethnic solidarity and so forth. Often people feel like they are part of a team so that when economic realities threaten to break up the team, the members come together and urge political measures that will protect their interests. The motivation may well be to express loyalty to those with whom they feel a closeness. This despite the fact that the protectionist measures impose considerable costs on many people who then will not have a chance to spend what they might have saved to create more jobs.

The recent upheavals in France exemplify this pretty clearly – so as to hang on to various costly benefits for the few, millions are kept from gaining jobs because protectionist measures keep investors from starting new enterprises. Artificial job security generates real unemployment.

In general, people are at odds with themselves about much of this – they like what's new and more efficient and satisfying but they also dislike when this brings change into their lives. And they are even willing to erect barriers that will prevent others from improving their lives just so the aggravating changes will be averted. No, they really have no right to do this, but the myth of the supreme rule of democracy blinds them to that fact, as if the principle of lynch mobs were OK except, well, when it comes to outright lynching.

What is needed is for folks to accept the fact that changes will occur and they will have to prepare for them. How? That is one of the questions they will have to answer and implement. The alternative is imposing stagnation and regress on all.

6.   COMPETITION – WHY SO HUMAN?

At Harvard University, a famous defender of communitarianism, Michael Sandel of the Department of Government, has denounced competition and reportedly has insisted that his own kids play only noncompetitive baseball. The reason? He believes that competition is too individualistic, supports a spirit of rivalry, and undermines the cooperative attitude that we should foster in ourselves.

At those times, when people are gearing up for the Olympic Games, we might as well pay some attention to Professor Sandel's lament and ask ourselves whether competition is or is not a good thing. And, as with so many matters, it will come to light that no "one-size-fits-all" answer is available to us. Nor, however, will we find that competition is some kind of human evil that has managed to infiltrate the human situation just to corrupt us all.

It will help to reflect for a moment on why some folks feel as Professor Sandel does. It comes from a view of human life that was nicely sketched by Karl Marx, namely, the belief that when humanity becomes fully mature, it will look something like a wonderful choir in which we all stand next to one another, wearing about the same outfit and harmonizing in a way that gives none of us a distinctive voice but merges all voices together into a single collective sound. It is this view that has excited the imagination of thousands of political thinkers, and it is one from which most have drawn their lesson of what is best for human beings as they try to flourish in their communities. It has also led, tragically, to massive totalitarian experiments in which people are coerced into a single mold that does violence to their human nature in the name of a misconceived dream.

A very pictorial illustration of this ideal comes to us from Communist China where, during Mao's rule, it was customary for millions of Chinese to march through the country together, all wearing identical-looking blue pajamas. (Never mind that the fabric of these garments revealed a serious class differentiation – that could not be seen as the world witnessed the Chinese spectacle.)

Instead of this image of humanity as one big, identically populated choir, the real story is quite another matter. We are much more different from one another than we are alike, and that is not just some temporary stage but the permanent condition of our human lives. We are significantly different in our biological make-up, and our free will leads us to make different decisions as we face the diverse circumstances of our lives. Most importantly, even where we face common circumstances, we often exert different levels of attention and effort, leading to different outcomes in our diverse lives.

As usual, there are symbolic ways that these basic facts are literally played out in human communities. The Olympic Games are the most visible and celebrated ways that we have come to register the spirit of competition in our lives. This competition is not at all the disharmonizing, acrimonious, alienating and hostile affair that critics make it out to be; quite the contrary. If you watch carefully, you will notice that the bulk of the events, quite like much of competitive life, are peaceful and even friendly, but demonstrative of the fact that human living requires close attention and much effort so that we may flourish at it. It may not be for everyone, either, this spirit of competition. But where it exists, it can be a show of human beings making the effort to do their best at some task.

In fact, competition isn't primarily a rivalry at all. That part of it may sometimes overshadow what is most important about it, namely, the mutual and harmonious effort to excel at something. Sure, the spectators and the promoters often stress the rivalry, but it would be a mistake to take that to be the essence of what is going on and what is being symbolically represented about human community life.

Competition is built into the fact of our individuality and mutual striving to make something of ourselves through the myriad of activities in which we take part. And apart from some cases of corruption – which, of course, can plague any aspect of human living – competition gives us a symbolic expression of one of life's realities, namely, that there is no guarantee of success and that everyone needs to work hard to get ahead but can do this with mutual respect and even in friendship. Competition, of course, is also spurred on by the fact of scarcity, as many economists would argue, although that's not sufficient for it to occur. After all, people are sometimes quite satisfied with exactly what they have and seek no more, certainly not necessarily something that is scarce (unless by 'scarce' is meant 'not available at the lowest conceivable price'). Sure, people often strive to obtain what others also want, and there may not be enough for all at a preferred price. In that case, they will need to engage in competitive bidding for it, so that someone can be selected as the winner.

But this is not the most basic reason for competition, which is that people want to do well, including doing well at obtaining economic benefits, and this leads to seeking advancement as best as they can, compared to others. After

all, much of competition is largely unrelated to economics – as exemplified by
athletics.

7.   REVISITING ZONING V. PRIVATE PROPERTY
RIGHTS

Among the elements of a free society, the institution of private property
rights looms very large. It is this element that gives concrete, practical expression to a citizen's right to liberty. Moreover, business would be impossible
without it – one cannot trade what one cannot own!

Generally, living free means doing what one chooses to do someplace, connected to the world around oneself. John Locke, the major theorist of individual rights in the history of political thought, believed that private property
rights punctuate our jurisdiction over our lives since what our lives amount to
is, to a large extent, interacting and mixing our labor with the rest of nature.
If we lack the right to private property, we lack the freedom to live on our
own terms.

No one who defends freedom suffers from the illusion that free men and
women always do what is right, and this is true about how they make use of
their property. But, in a genuinely free society, that is one of the troubling yet
unavoidable conditions of living with other people. Just as one is, so are others
free to use what belongs to them as they judge proper. If this is undermined,
so is human freedom.

One of the areas in community life where this element of freedom is often
evaded and opposed is the institution of zoning ordinances. Zoning amounts to
the regulation of one's ability to use one's land and home and business as one
judges fit, in favor of how others do. In a democratic society, these 'others'
are usually representatives of the majority, although very often they become
nearly independent agents who can dictate the ways land and buildings must
be built, decorated, rebuilt, and so forth. The justification offered for this, as
for most other violations of private property rights, has to do with protecting
the members of the majority from the choices of members of the minority,
choices that the majority would find objectionable. Thus the typical announced
objective of a zoning ordinance is to preserve the styles that the majority of the
community prefers within a neighborhood, and to keep out undesirable colors
and architectural styles, not to mention business establishments and lifestyles.

All this is usually put in terms of establishing and maintaining community
standards, of course, as if there were such a thing as the community apart from
all of its members. But there isn't. So what is left is some members of the
community deciding for all the members how private property will be used. In
effect, of course, this means the abolition of private property rights, that great
goal that was first on the list of Karl Marx's and Frederick Engels's *Communist*

Manifesto. Sure, defenders of zoning laws will insist that they simply want to protect the private properties of members of the neighborhood against those who would undermine property values, and the desirability of the vicinity as a residential, commercial or industrial region. However, whatever their motives, these defenders are still working to undermine – and have been succeeding at undermining – the institution of private property rights.

You see, a right is a freedom to do what one wants, be this good or bad, provided no one's rights are violated in the process. Freedom of speech, for example, means one may say anything one wants that amounts to speech, provided it does not violate another's rights. What is said could be filthy, false, offensive, unwise, and so forth. But free men and women may not be stopped from speaking out, whatever the quality of their speech.

Perhaps it appears to many that freedom of speech is more important than property rights, but this is easily disproved. Indeed, without private property rights, there cannot be freedom of speech. The community would own or control all places where things could be said and published, and thus, also, what can be said and published. (This is why, for example, government can regulate television and radio content but not that of magazines and newspapers. The BBC, for example, banned Churchill in the late 1930s and, of course, PBS and NPR, all tied in with government, are very selective in what viewpoints they air. And even in commercial broadcasting, the government 'owns' the electromagnetic spectrum on which signals travel, so governments can impose many rules on those who use this medium!)

But perhaps, in the case of certain kinds of property, such as land and buildings, the borders between what one person owns and others own cannot be determined, so there really cannot be any private property rights applicable in such spheres. There seems to be something to this. mainly because many people think that when they own a piece of land or a house, the surrounding views also belong to them – or at least they ought to have a say as to what happens to whatever is in view. (The famous Chicago economist and law professor Ronald Coase had argued that it doesn't matter who owns what, so long as ownership is identified and kept consistent. But this is clearly false – it matters to those whose ownership rights are at stake.)

If one's neighbor is a nice-looking person but then decides not to remain nice-looking, one has no right to stop the person from changing, however disappointing this may be to one. Indeed, this is true about another's automobile, backyard, and so forth. And that should be the model on which to base our understanding of private property – those who own it must have control over it; otherwise, they aren't free persons but belong to other people who claim to represent the community.

So what now? If zoning ordinances violate certain valid principles of a free society, how can one nevertheless work to keep one's neighborhood presentable? How can one influence, if not control, other people so that they do not make the neighborhood unpleasant and allow it to deteriorate?

So far I have tried to show in rather general terms why zoning laws are inconsistent with a free society's principles, in particular with the principle of private property rights. Basically, they amount to the imposition by some people on others of conditions for using property that are the owners' proper, justified authority to determine. No one has that right, however tempting and desirable it may appear to imagine otherwise.

But what about the perfectly honorable wish to have a nice neighborhood in which to live, work and play? How, besides by means of zoning ordinances, could people protect their neighborhoods?

Before answering this question, it must be noted, quite emphatically, that zoning ordinances by no means achieve what their advocates claim justifies their use. Indeed, in many communities that have stringent zoning ordinances, there are neighborhoods that are a mess, to put it mildly. Especially right where the zoning provisions change, say from commercial to residential use, the areas are usually in a deteriorating condition. That is where buildings are usually dilapidated, shabby. And it is usually those who lack political clout who must live there.

In more general terms, by no means is the institution of zoning laws a panacea. Just as with the welfare state in general, which simply shoves around the misery it aims to eliminate, zoning laws are mostly an expression of special-interest clout. A drive through any of the heavily zoned communities will demonstrate this, right away.

In fact, the record of the institution of zoning, as far as making areas of residential, commercial and recreational living orderly and pleasant for all, is by no means a good one. Let us look at this briefly, without entering into the ample scholarship that exists on that topic. (But anyone wishing to check for detailed studies can examine William A. Fishel's works, *Regulatory Takings: Law, Economics, and Politics, Do Growth Controls Matter?: A Review of Empirical Evidence on the Effectiveness and Efficiency of Local Government Land Use Regulation; The Economics of Zoning Laws: A Property Rights Approach to American Land Use Controls*, and *Land Economics: Private Markets Public Decisions*, as well as Bernard H. Siegan's seminal book, *Land Use Without Zoning*. Finally, there is Steven Greenhut's previously mentioned fine book, *Abuse of Power*.)

For one, there is a city in the USA that has enjoyed freedom from zoning and has worked pretty well, so far. It is Houston, Texas. No disaster, no catastrophe, no mess, no property devaluation, nada. Just a city where what zoning was supposed to achieve has been achieved without it, more peacefully, more through cooperation than through coercion.

Second, a little imagination and history should suffice to teach us all that it is better all around to strive to achieve goals without forcing people to accept what they would freely reject. And this applies as much to education or military service as it does to not keeping their neighborhoods in good shape. Free men and women simply do better, on the whole, than do those who are regimented by their fellows and made to act as they do not choose.

Third, what zoning aims for can easily be achieved through voluntary agreements among members of neighborhoods. Restrictive covenants work to this end wonderfully, provided those concerned make the effort to bring them into play. As with all things, the free approach always appears cumbersome, at first – talking someone into a course of conduct takes more time than doing this by coercing the person. But in the end, the result is much more rewarding – all kinds of political hostilities, vested-interest battles, and politicking in the worst sense of that term can be avoided if agreements are reached peacefully, through mutual effort – e.g., via home owners associations.

Of course, in most communities this is at best an ideal, or more likely a political fantasy, along the lines that abolishing prohibition had been at one time, and that substituting a private for a public education system is now. But that does not make it any less feasible and right! So, in the current dispute about whether this or that kind of zoning ordinance is needed for a community, it is vital that some voices keep announcing what is the truly best solution, after all.

What is needed, once all the infighting has betrayed itself as the fruitless effort it really is, is the abolition of zoning and the institution of market-based, voluntary agreements among members of neighborhoods, commercial establishments and so forth, to achieve what these members want to achieve. There will, of course, be limits to what is possible – one cannot live in Shangri-La if one isn't financially equipped to do so; one cannot live deep in the woods if one's budget provides for only an apartment in the middle of town. But within the limits that one must live with in all realms of ordinary life, the solutions reached via voluntary negotiations and bargaining are far superior to those acrimonious ones that are reached via the political process.

Will this be done tomorrow morning at 9 AM? No. But should we stress its desirability and real availability for any community? Yes.

Chapter 3

BUSINESS AND CAPITALISM

1. WHY CAPITALISM ISN'T FULLY EMBRACED

When the Soviet empire finally collapsed, many people, especially in the West, were filled with unreasonable expectations. Journalists in particular demanded an instant revitalization of Eastern European economies, the flowering of business, investments, a rise in the standard of living, vigorous entrepreneurship everywhere, exploration of natural resources, and, most of all, the establishment of a legal framework for all of this, throughout the region.

Although prices have been deregulated in various countries, the needed reforms in property and contract law are still a long way off. The political will and conviction needed to produce them is not in evidence anywhere in the region, apart from the Czech Republic – certainly Bulgaria, Russia, and Poland do not appear to be headed toward the establishment of legal instruments that facilitate the development of *bona fide* free markets.

This has even prompted such big financial market players as George Soros to turn away from capitalism and embrace a so-called open society that is really just the old-fashioned mixed economy, which, as Hungarian economist Janos Kornai warned in *The Road to the Free Market Economy* (W. W. Norton & Co Inc 1990), cannot be supported until a society has generated significant wealth.

Socialism and the idealization of communism are by no means the only obstacles to economic health in Eastern Europe. More deep-seated is the enduring hostility toward business.

This is not new. Throughout human history, prominent thinkers and theologians have decried commerce and trade as lowly, base, and ignoble. Plato had Socrates place merchants at the lowest rung of society in *The Republic*; Aristotle believed that wealth creation was never a source of genuine human goodness; in Islam, the concern with the afterlife often leads to hostility toward efforts to secure prosperity in this one; Christianity says that sooner will the camel go through the eye of the needle than the rich man gain entrance to the kingdom of Heaven; the practice of money lending with interest was regarded as usury until very recently; and even business in the so-called capitalist

United States is regulated by government in ways that members of the clergy or the press would never tolerate if subjected to such regulation themselves.[18]

Artists, politicians, philosophers, theologians, movie scriptwriters, poets, and lyricists rarely have anything nice to say about business and commerce.

But everyone would like to be rich. What schizophrenia! Men and women all over the world clamor to be better off, financially, while the ideas propagated by most intellectuals and moral leaders in their societies denounce that very desire. Nowhere is this contradiction more evident than in the former Soviet colonies.

Although people throughout this region longingly eye the wealth of countries where business and industry have experienced some measure of freedom, they nearly always express disdain and even contempt for those who actively, ambitiously enter the commercial world. They condemn such people as speculators and exploiters, and those who witness their success are resentful – though often envious.

This has to be stopped. But how? First of all, one must abandon the labor theory of value – the idea that only the kind of work in which people sweat is real work that deserves reward. Most worthwhile work is actually a matter of good judgment, figuring out what people want badly enough and then making sure it is produced for them at a reasonable price. Business acumen is a matter of intelligence, so it is often not directly observable. Successful businesspeople use their minds to earn their millions – though, of course, as with everything, luck has its place there, too.

But even more in need of remedial thinking is a matter that has led to the condemnation of business. The human race has always been ambivalent about where a person really belongs – here on earth or somewhere else, in some other realm, nearer to God, perhaps.

Well, we are here, and this is where we have some say about how we live. If there is an afterlife, there is little anyone actually knows about it.

The best thing for everyone to do would be to focus clearly on what it takes to make something out of this life. And 'this life' clearly includes a hefty economic dimension: that is how children get better shoes and education, families a good vacation or dental care, and anyone a safe and comfortable car. Even high culture is easily accessed if one is able to afford it. Books, music, theater, and the rest are all going to come our way more readily if we work hard to earn a decent living.

It is businesspeople who can provide us with the service of increasing our wealth – carefully and cautiously, depending on one's situation, responsibilities, and talents. It is this profession that secures the health of our bankbooks,

---

[18]Perhaps this also explains why prostitutes are punished more severely than "Johns."

so we should treat it with no less respect than the doctors and dentists who secure the health of our bodies.

Businesspeople in Eastern Europe need respect from society comparable to that received by educators, scientists, artists, and physicians. Then they can go to work with pride, and embark on the difficult task of revitalizing the stagnant, defeated economic culture that was produced by an ideology that thought of those in business as the scum of the earth.

It is, in short, not enough simply to say an official good-bye to the anti-business mentality of the Communist Era. It is necessary, at the same time, to establish a newfound respect for the profession of business, one that will gradually teach those who embark on business – of whom, let us hope, there will be many – that they are doing something worthwhile, honorable, and respectable.

With that psychological, even spiritual support, the economies of numerous formerly communist countries where progress is still stagnant can begin to improve and, in time, even flourish.[19]

2.   A PANIC ABOUT FREEDOM?

The New York Times uses "Choose Capitalism" as its headline for a profile on the previous Chinese premier who presided over the recent surge toward some measure of liberty in the People's Republic of China. The implication? He and his cohorts actually made a deliberate decision to introduce capitalist elements into China's economy.

The Atlantic Monthly features billionaire George Soros, who makes reference to and laments, in an article titled "The Threat of Capitalism," the "intensification of laissez-faire capitalism and the spread of market values into all areas of life." The implication? The globe is now in the throes of economic liberty everywhere, and it is something to be feared and dreaded.

Newsweek, in reviewing books by two severe critics of free-market economics, Robert Kuttner and William Greider, announces that capitalism is now "our secular religion." The implication is that our culture is populated by millions and millions of citizens who accept, on blind faith, the soundness of a free-market economy.

What is happening here? When such exaggerations can pass for serious news headlines and analysis, it probably isn't an accident. Something is going

---

[19]Growth, of course, is on the rise, although in somewhat paradoxical ways. Consider tobacco: farmers get off free but cigarette companies are severely condemned; convenience stores that sell cigarettes are fine; smokers are victims; but advertisers of tobacco products are evil or harmless, depending on the culture in which they run their ads. All this may require some in-depth discussion of just how nuanced the anti-capitalist mentality may be.

on, although not what a cursory reading of these various published missives would suggest.

No, China has no capitalist economy, albeit its unprincipled leaders realize that classical socialism isn't getting them anywhere and it is best to introduce certain elements of free-market economics, even while political and economic power are still held by an elite.

No, the world is not in the grip of capitalist developments everywhere. The facts of life, however, cannot be ignored in an age when the media is blasting the news from every corner of the globe so no one can evade the facts about the demise of centrally dictated economic systems and what havoc they wreak over the lives of millions.

No, most Americans do not worship capitalism. But, of course – apart from the bulk of intellectuals who are enamored by the Platonic ideal of an intellectually regimented society and who are, in most cases, in the employ of politically managed educational institutions – most Americans still exhibit the gut sense that a competitive, free market is a better way to organize economic affairs than is any tinkering, meddling statist economic order.

So then why are all these media outfits spreading distortions? Why pretend that capitalism rules the world and Americans have blind faith in it?

3.   THE "CRITICAL" ANALYSIS

Soros, we must note, has never been a champion of free market capitalism. He has followed for nearly all his public life the political ideas of the late Sir Karl Popper who laid out a rather jumbled case for what he dubbed "the open society" in his *The Open Society and Its Enemies* (1953). Such a society is what we ordinarily call the pragmatic system in which politicians get involved in people's lives but without any heavy theoretical machinery to guide them, simply as the ad hoc parental authorities who are believed to be needed to keep us all on the straight and narrow. Popper was at one time a Marxist socialist but became disillusioned with that idea because he came to believe that systematic ideas do not work in any area of human concern.

The Popperian open society Soros promotes is characterized by a very general policy of having no firm principles, not even those needed for it to have some constancy and integrity. This makes the open society a rather wobbly idea, since even what Popper himself regarded as central to all human thinking, critical rationalism, may be undermined by the openness of the open society since its main target is negative: avoid dogmatic thinking, and avoid anything that even comes close to a set of unbreachable principles. No, the open society is open to anything at all, at least for experimental purposes. No holds are barred, which, if you think about it, undermines even that very idea and becomes unworkable.

Accordingly, in a society Soros regards suited to human community living, the state can manipulate many aspects of human life, including, of course, the economic behavior of individuals and firms. It can control the money supply, impose wage and price controls, dabble in demand or supply-side economics, and do nearly everything a central planning board might – provided it does not settle into any one policy firmly, unbendingly. That is the gist of Soros's Popperian politics.[20]

Soros' distrusts capitalism in particular, because of the alleged inadequacy of neo-classical economics, the technical economic underpinnings of capitalist thinking offered up in many university economics departments. He, like many others outside and even inside the economics discipline, finds the arid reductionism of this social science false to the facts, and rightly so. But the defense of capitalist free markets does not rest on this position.

Neo-classical thinking depends in large part on the 18th- and 19th-century belief that human society operates according to laws, not unlike those that govern the physical universe. Most of social science embraced that faith, so economics isn't unusual in its loyalty to classical mechanics. Nor do all economists take the deterministic lawfulness of economic science literally – some understand that the laws begin to operate only once people embark upon economic pursuits. Outside their commercial ventures, people can follow different principles and priorities, even if it is undeniable that most of their endeavors have economic features. Yet, it would be foolish to construe religion or romance or even scientific inquiry as solely explicable by reference to the laws of economics.

In his criticism of neo-classical economic science, then, George Soros has a point: the discipline is too dependent on Newtonian physics as the model of science. As a result, the predictions of economists who look at markets as if they were machines need to be taken with a grain of salt.

Some – for example the school of Austrian economists – have made exactly that point against the neo-classicals. But Soros does not even acknowledge that among economists who favor a free market there is dispute on the very issues he raises. Some accept the criticism and yet also champion laissez-faire, which he himself considers dogmatic – for example, Ludwig von Mises.

Soros draws a mistaken inference: if one defense of the market is flawed, the market lacks defense. This is wrong. If it is true that from A we can infer B, it does not prove that B can only be inferred from A; C or Z, too, might be a reason for B.

---

[20]It was state dabbling in exchange control in Thailand that enabled Soros to reap millions, while exposing the faults of government intervention, the very kind he supports!

For example, aside from what economics teaches us, there are moral arguments for the free-market system resting on the idea of individual rights to life, liberty and the pursuit of happiness. Soros appears to be oblivious to this.

Robert Kuttner, of course, is a traditional welfare statist verging on socialism. He just does not like the hustle bustle of the free market, the fact that it has winners and losers at the margins, that some folks aren't going to be taken care of, no matter what, because in free societies people are also free to be unkind, ungenerous. This is the gist of most of the criticisms of capitalism, especially when that system is linked, rather unfairly, with the thought of Herbert Spencer's Social Darwinism. The first who made the case along these lines was John Maynard Keynes, in his 1926 book *The End of Laissez-Faire*. Kuttner actually wrote a book with that very same title, a few years back.

Some economists may hold, as my colleague Don Booth does, that "capitalism is a set of rules on how to compete; there is no alternative to competition; violence is a form of competition."[21] This is to overstate things a bit – violence is anti-competitive since it most often disables prospective competitors from taking part in the competitive enterprise. Also, capitalism does not actually require competition. As the late Robert Nozick noted, capitalism – or libertarianism – makes possible experimentation in a variety of social arrangements, some of which, such as those involving communes or the kibbutz, do not involve competition at all.

In any case, the idea behind the Keynes-Kuttner stance is that only the government is powerful, reliable, and virtuous enough to rescue us all from the evils of a mean-minded, hard-hearted marketplace. Only with good folks in Washington, Sacramento, Albany, Bonn, or Moscow will we have some decency injected in the midst of all that nasty, cut-throat competition that we find in free markets. Capitalism, while needed to supply us with food and shelter, cannot be left to the people taking part in it – outsiders who are wise and virtuous need to tame it.

4.   THE ANALYSIS IS ASKEW

Soros's Popperian view is flawed because it starts with a bad premise, namely, that we cannot know anything for sure. No view that starts this way can be defended, since in defending it one is contradicting it. What kind of defense could be offered for something that says nothing can be well-enough defended to survive challenges? Indeed, Popper himself vacillates between being nearly dogmatic about his views and mouthing the principles of "critical rationalism," that is, that everything is open to doubt.

---

[21] Personal correspondence.

In reply we can say that Soros's mistake is to fail to appreciate just how open an open society must be. It cannot be closed, period, because this will stymie the very process Soros and Popper love so much, criticism. Government planning, setting of minimum wages, regulating commerce and industry – all of this, unless it is done to punish transgressors of just laws, counts as impeding criticism, the input-output mechanism of a system of free human commercial interaction. Free markets are the paradigm of critical rationalism in action! Once the state starts setting its standards, criticism is dead, power begins to rule, and the result is stagnation, the closing off of opportunities for newcomers, especially, and the protection of the established against the striving.

Quite apart from Soros's concerns, it is important that economics take into account the fact that human beings have free will and can act, at least temporarily, contrary to the law of supply and demand: they may just refuse to be prudent and may act against their best economic interest; they may lie back and not take part in market competition; they may decline the chance to prosper.

Soros goes astray when he relies on Popperian thinking. Critical rationalism leaves open the issue of where the standards of criticism, the criteria for judging things, are to be located. If everything is open to doubt, how can one even criticize? Here is a serious lacuna in Popperian politics, as well as science, and Soros should not embrace it without being more critical of it. Instead, Soros appears to reject any principled approach to politics quite uncritically, leaving his thinking about the subject to rest on quicksand instead of on something solid enough to serve as a framework for analysis and criticism.

5. WHAT EXACTLY IS A FREE, CAPITALIST SYSTEM?

In general, it is crucial to call to mind that free-market capitalism or laissez-faire is an economic organization wherein individuals embark upon various ventures – production, exchange, insurance, invention, investment, saving, speculation, etc. – on their own initiative, and free of government interventions such as barrier to entry, regulation of prices and wages, and imposition of non-contractually determined standards of employment and trade. In short, we are talking here of a *bona fide* free society, the organization and continuation of which requires a legal system that takes both personal/civil liberties and private property rights extremely seriously.

Indeed, the major and most distinguished defenders of this kind of economic order – such as Ludwig von Mises, F. A. Hayek, Milton Friedman – or its broader political-legal framework of libertarianism – such as Ayn Rand, Robert Nozick, Anthony Flew, John Hospers, et al. – have insisted that there really cannot be a capitalist system without the consistent establishment and maintenance of a society that protects individual rights to life, liberty and property, one that treats individual citizens as sovereign and fully responsible for their own conduct.

As others have already noted, Soros's lament should be focused not on capitalism but on the mixed-up, perverse systems of the former Soviet colonies, which lack any of the legal preconditions needed for capitalism to succeed. Where the laws of property and contract are entirely primitive, and any development of them is widely resisted by the still active communists in the governments, no peaceful pursuit of profit or *bona fide* competitive enterprise is possible. Instead, what we witness is a free-for-all which is at the mercy of criminal elements that substitute in violent and arbitrary ways for the conditions of a *bona fide* free-market society.

6.   THE SYSTEM IS POSSIBLE BUT NOT IN EFFECT

So no capitalist system exists anywhere, not even in the West, where we find mostly mixed economies with steadily expanding government intervention. Nor is even the *idea* of free-market capitalism gaining much acceptance, either in the USA or elsewhere in the world. What we witness is a desperate effort to combine incompatible features of drastically varied political economies.

What may mislead some folks, such as George Soros, is that here and there, especially since the fall of the USSR and its utterly defunct centrally planned socialist economy, various countries have been instituting privatization, whereby many state functions are partially farmed out to private enterprise. Many countries have reduced the scale of involvement of their governments in manufacturing and selling goods and services, and in banking and investing, at least on some fronts. They have often abolished central planning of the economy, although this has by no means been extended to that all-important area of the monetary system, which is almost everywhere firmly in the hands of central banks and federal reserve boards. Yet, without a system of free banking, the free market is not fully realizable.

So is the movement toward partial privatization enough for us to consider the changes as an "untrammeled intensification of laissez-faire," to quote Mr. Soros? No. If there were such an intensification, then perhaps more folks throughout the world would have a genuine crack at becoming billionaires, and Mr. Soros would have many more savvy competitors, all of whom would be going after big bucks, unimpeded by state bureaucracies. In fact, what most societies in the former Soviet colonies have done is to change into sloppy welfare states – usually to their peril. (That, incidentally, was predicted by Janos Kornai, the Hungarian economist; his *The Road to the Free Market Economy* made clear that 'welfarism' will bring the newly liberated systems to their knees, since they haven't the economic strength to support massive doses of

Robin Hoodism.) And that, combined with their lack of a suitable legal base for genuine capitalism, has generated a new set of problems that have nothing to do with any threat of capitalism.

7. NO GLOBAL WAVE OF RADICAL CAPITALISM

So there really isn't anything close to a free-market system spreading across the globe, even while some of the features of free markets are, of course, in far greater abundance than just a few decades ago. Yet, everywhere, governments are still major agents of economic decision making, owning massive territories and other wealth in their respective countries, imposing huge tax burdens on every entrepreneur who dares to make a buck or two from honest trade (while often leaving the organized gangs of thieves and murderers, who have no respect for individual rights, to run amuck in their land). But why, then, do we find such a plethora of overstatements about the imminence of capitalism?

Some may actually think capitalism is a menace – I think George Soros does so because he is guided in his thinking by Popper's antipathy toward any kind of politics based on principles, never mind the content of those principles. He also mistakes the criminal anarchy of some of the old Soviet economies for a type of capitalism, which is simply uninformed.

Many others may be upset with even the slight respectability that capitalism has gained in the recent past, if only because of socialism's dismal failure. This position has a very deep, ancient basis for the low regard in which commerce and business have been held throughout human history, nearly everywhere around the globe.

The bulk of intellectuals have tended, at least thus far, to embrace the idea that paying too much attention to earthly joys and happiness, something that business and capitalism – which is very hospitable to business – help to support, is a lowly objective in life. Plato, Aristotle, Augustine, and the rest, with only a few exceptions, and nearly all the members of the American Philosophical Association who give the matter any attention at all, find capitalism loathsome. Many regard it with as much hatred as Fascism and Nazism, and most clearly find socialism, its opposite, to be a humane and decent alternative, by comparison. Never mind that it has failed wherever it has been tried – as an ideal, it rules the minds of most of the professional thinkers around the globe.

This is fact, not myth. Any perusal of books from major university publishing houses will confirm it. Bookstores near every important university give ample evidence – the shelves are filled with Marxist and Marxist-derivative political and social philosophy. The only exception is the discipline of economics, which most detractors regard as a kind of handmaiden of capitalism.

Even then, most of the economists do not defend the morality of the system, only its efficiency for the purpose of generating wealth. (Of course, there is much to be said for this, unless you are an intellectual who is inclined to think that suffering and poverty are the means to moral purification.) Just take a look at the social and political philosophy or business ethics textbooks assigned to students throughout higher education! Examine what is said about business and capitalism. (I have done this, with my colleague Professor Douglas J. Den Uyl, in the *American Philosophical Quarterly,* Vol. 24 [April 1987], pp. 107–124.) The system is nearly universally despised. Poor Ayn Rand suffered because she, a refugee from the Soviet Union, found great merit in it. The rest of us in academic philosophy who have found merit in capitalism have had to work double- and triple-time to make ourselves heard over the chorus of anti-capitalist rhetoric and scholarship, with hardly any publisher touching our works except some on the fringes that serve select audiences.

8.   A PUZZLE

Why do *The Atlantic Monthly, Harper's, Newsweek* and other publications serve up all these criticisms of capitalism just now? That is a mystery. Perhaps they all find the system a *bona fide* menace to human community life. But there is nothing new about that – most intellectuals haven't liked it, for over a century. It may be naïve to think that all of this clamor to find fault with capitalism is a matter of honest intellectual exchange.

But the vigorous publication of nothing but the attacks on capitalism in *The Atlantic, Harper's, Newsweek*, etc., raises some questions about motivations, questions that cannot be answered without knowing more about the publishers and editors involved. Even if they were all entirely honest, sincere – merely worried about the alleged dangers or excesses of a fully free society – it wouldn't make their charges acceptable, for what they target for their misguided attacks happens to be the most promising system of political economy that the human mind has ever conceived. No, it is no utopia; thus, one will be able to point to human misadventures, misfortunes, and dissatisfactions in its (hypothetical) midst, yet far less so than in the midst of any other live option.

It is a shame to spend so much energy attacking what is ultimately the most human, moral and productive system of economics we have experienced in human history.

9.   SECULARISM AND CAPITALISM

When Ayn Rand entered the American cultural stage with her novels, *The Fountainhead* (1943) and *Atlas Shrugged* (1957), it surprised some of her fans that American conservatives received her with scorn rather than cheers.

National Review ran a vicious screed against *Atlas Shrugged*, by the ex-communist-turned-devoted-Christian Whittaker Chambers; William F. Buckley, Jr., began his life-long belittling of her fiction and ideas – he reproduces such an essay in several of his books – and in general the conservative intelligentsia disowned her without much study of her thought.

All this despite the fact that Rand became one of the most avid supporters of American capitalism, defending this political economic system from a full-fledged philosophical-moral framework she called Objectivism. Why did her efforts inspire such disdain from conservatives?

The answer is rather straightforward. Rand was an avowed atheist. She had no use for anything supernatural, anything mystical, or anything that was in principle inaccessible to human understanding. She saw no justification for belief in a divine supreme being in metaphysics, let alone in science, none at all. And for this she paid dearly. She is still dismissed or, more often now, treated with disdain by many of those who consider themselves champions of American capitalism and free-market economics, including many of the economists who are at the forefront, and rather alone, in the defense of this system within the academy. (Although there are signs of change – the prestigious Cato Institute in Washington, DC, recently held a huge bash on the occasion of the anniversary of the publication of *Atlas Shrugged*.)

The Left, too, disliked Rand, mainly because of her unabashed (some would say "in your face") support of America's founding principles and of capitalism. She didn't make many friends, either, with her non-fiction titles, such as *The Virtue of Selfishness* (1961) and *Capitalism: The Unknown Ideal* (1967). Her first two novels, *We the Living* (1936) and *Anthem* (1938), which didn't become popular until after the next one hit the bestseller lists, had been rather direct attacks on the Left's favorite experiment in utopianism, the Soviet Union, so it was no surprise that there was no love for her work emanating from their circles.

I tell this story not so much to feature Ayn Rand but to use her case to illustrate an interesting aspect of contemporary political theory and geopolitics. Ever since Osama bin Laden unleashed his venom and suicide troops against the United States of America, especially the men and women who worked in the World Trade Center – using as ammunition, in part, the innocent passengers and crew on non-military transport planes – there has been a lot of hand-wringing about just why so many in the Islamic world have it in for the USA. It is notable that, shortly after September 11, 2001, President Bush, a political hero to most American conservatives, went on record claiming that it isn't Islam per se that sees us in such a dark light but some renegade versions of that faith. A good many people followed him in this so that, over time, it became a refrain on the Right that Islam is peaceful and gentle, except for some of the crazier versions of it.

Yet, as subsequent work has shown – see, especially, Robert Spencer's *Islam Unveiled* (Encounter, 2002) and Paul Berman's *Terror and Liberalism* (Norton, 2003) – a good deal of what the Koran says suggests that Islam as such, not just its fundamentalist or extremist varieties, finds grave fault with the public philosophy of the USA and much of the West.

Islam is, in fact, a fiercely otherworldly theology, one that sees absolutely no distinction between what is due to God versus what is due to Caesar. State and church are ideally the same, just as we have seen played out in the state of Iran ever since the Shah was ousted and the Ayatollahs took over the reins of government. Elsewhere, too, the secularization of countries with sizable Muslim populations has been arrested – even Turkey, the most secular of the nations with Muslim populations, hasn't quite managed to rid itself of the threat of such an interpretation of the Koran, and Egypt, among others, continues to find it difficult to manage the problems this causes.

Of course, there are nuances to the various renditions of Islam, just as there are to all faiths and philosophies, but the gist of the difference between Islam and the West is that Islam takes the supernatural world far more seriously, both in theory and practice, than do most prominent contemporary Christian religions and theologies. One of the most important consequences of the Islamic position is that the state is seen as a direct instrument for regimenting virtue within its realm. Virtuous *behavior* is the goal and, in contrast to modern Christianity, Islam has no commitment to the idea that the faithful must *voluntarily choose* to embrace the moral virtues and, indeed, the faith itself.

In fact, it is this latter element of Christianity that is arguably responsible for the co-existence between Western secular-liberal public philosophies and the West's various theological systems. Not that it has always been that way; quite the contrary, although the humanity of Jesus has tended to moderate the otherworldliness of Christianity, as has Aquinas's combination of the faith with Aristotelianism in the 13th century AD.

Still, although most Roman Catholics today will insist that the Holy Inquisition was an aberration, it is clear that acceptance and compliance with the doctrines of the Catholic faith had at one time been thought to be achievable via coercion. (Although even there the idea was to "persuade" people to choose – via coerced confession – to accept the faith, albeit with methods that left little room for genuine free choice.) Today, however, most Western faiths have made some kind of peace with the liberal political tradition, one that developed, after all – say, in the writings of John Locke – in large measure by thinking through the relationship between state and church and tolerance in general.

At bottom, however, Islam and Christianity do in fact share their mutual devotion to the supernatural realm, spiritualism, the afterlife and everlasting salvation. They both cherish the idea that life on Earth is but a stepping stone to a much richer kind of life, one that eschews completely the attachment to material reality. "Materialism" is, after all, a contemptible system in the view of both schools of theology, albeit with Christianity managing some kind of mishmash between its kind of Spiritualism and Materialism. (Islam, of course, has also managed to achieve such a reconciliation in the practical lives of many Muslims – no one can argue, in good faith, that all Saudi Muslims are living primarily, let alone exclusively, spiritual lives!)

Much of this has been discussed in considerable detail since September 11, 2001, but one thing has managed to be left nearly unmentioned. This is that the charge, leveled at the USA by bin Laden and his cohorts, is substantially correct: Capitalism is intimately connected with the materialist, naturalist or secular aspects of the West.

Consider it in the simplest of all respects: If no afterlife exists for which we are ethically required to prepare, there is utterly no point in believing that earthly riches are superfluous. Quite the contrary; living well during one's sixty-odd years is all there is one can reasonably hope for and to strive to make this possible with the strong aid of tradable assets, as the rationale for capitalism stresses, is indeed a worthy undertaking.

To put the matter even more succinctly, the World Trade Center towers did, in fact, accurately symbolize the essence of what distinguishes Islam from Western liberalism, when rightly understood. It is via commerce that human beings living a relatively short (but still only) life can make much of their existence. It is riches that enable us to purchase food and travel, and to facilitate a good deal of all the rest, such as family life, friendship, scholarship, art and so forth. The poor are right to lament being poor because, as even Karl Marx noted, they have nothing more to look forward to, no afterlife in which they will find full consolation for their earthbound misery.

Capitalism is arguably – especially after the notorious collapse of the socialist experiment of the Soviet Union – the political economic system that best serves the goal of enriching ourselves in this life. Most secularists do not wish to admit this fact – indeed, a great many secular humanists, starting with Auguste Comte and the early Marx himself, hold out hope for some kind of viable anti-capitalist political economy, even if it isn't centrally planned socialism but some substitute such as market socialism and communitarianism. (Even Ludwig Feuerbach's version of materialistic humanism promised to translate Christian ideals into secular terms, thus betraying itself for the reactionary doctrine it was.)

Many leaders of modern radical Islam correctly see this as fantasy. They recognize in capitalism their nemesis, one that Christianity, they contend, is too feeble to subdue, tame, or in some other way set on the right track.

The uncomfortable news for secular humanists is that, while they do represent the most advanced philosophical thinking about human life, they are still clinging to a defunct political economy, namely, one in which the supreme importance of profit-making – in other words, of prosperity – is denied, even scorned. For them, the sad news is that Ayn Rand was right.

Capitalism is the right political economic system for a natural species such as humanity, one in which individual members, in contrast to those of other natural species, must forge their own plans in life, including their own system of community life, so as to flourish to the highest possible degree as the kind of – namely, human – beings that they are.

10. SOME NEGLECTED REASONS FOR CAPITALISM

"Why," many have asked and have attempted to answer, "does Western-style capitalism, and business in general, fail to engender loyalty, especially from intellectuals?" The great majority of those who work at universities and colleges, at least since the late 60s, but even before, have been hostile to capitalism, even while socialism and political economic systems with extensive government regulation have been shown to be unworkable as engines of prosperity. In the humanities and social sciences, this is glaringly evident, but even in economics there are great numbers of scholars who favor considerable government intervention in the economy.

This is the theme of Professor Dwight Lee, of the University of Georgia, in his contribution, "The Persistence of Socialism on Campus," to a very interesting book, *The Visible Hand, The Challenges to Private Enterprise in the 21st Century* (RCPE Book, 2000). He explores why academicians tend, to an amazingly large degree, to be socialists of one stripe or another.

I have co-authored, with Professor James Chesher, the book *The Business of Commerce, Examining An Honorable Profession* (Hoover Institution Press, 1999), in which this is one of the central topics. We deal, mainly, with the intellectual history of opposition to commerce, business and capitalism, examining what the view of commerce and business has been in the main philosophical and theological traditions throughout the West (and to some extent the East).

One point, worth revisiting, that we stress in the book is something Professor Lee does not discuss, namely, why commerce, business and, therefore, capitalism are morally or ethically demeaned. Why do both the academy – as well as Hollywood and the media – and especially the most prestigious institutions continue to besmirch business and capitalism? What is it in the history of ideas that most contributes to this attitude on the part of too many thinking people?

Very briefly put, in much of Western and indeed Eastern culture, there is and has been a philosophical-theological orientation favoring the supernatural, or at least the mental dimension – the spiritual or ideal realm or reality (as per Plato and many others) – which has painted nature in an inferior light. Commerce, business and capitalism, in turn, have always been acknowledged to be directed toward improving our earthly lot, so they have been looked upon as lowly, base, or ignoble. Clearly, this has favored the ideas and ideals that take us either into some abstract or a supernatural realm.

Even secular thinking has adopted this stance, albeit in a somewhat different guise – in Marxism, for example, the highest life is one of criticism and intellectualism, which is what everyone would be involved in once communism is achieved and labor has been taken over by machines. (Therefore, the usual Marxist kudos toward labor are disingenuous – ultimately, it is the intellectual whose life is most honored by Marx, much as it was for Socrates, Plato and Aristotle. This is just another way of favoring the spiritual dimension of human life.) From all of this, we get the ethics that disparage practical, ordinary life and its aspirations, hopes, pleasures and joys and, most of all, the virtue of prudence that guides us to success in the practical realm. Indeed, as I argued earlier, ever since the 17th century, prudence had been viewed as not being a virtue at all, but a drive we must tame by means of our higher faculties. That is what the great German philosopher Immanuel Kant taught, and what the bulk of moral philosophers and ethicists now tend to believe – practical things will take care of themselves (we have instincts for that), and morality must focus on striving for nearly impossible ideals (like perfect equality, fairness and social justice).

Thus the broader philosophical-theological framework of most cultures across the globe, and the morality that is grounded on this framework, stands against the idea that we should look with favor upon commerce, business and the system most hospitable to these, capitalism. Sure, as far as being well off, creating wealth, combating poverty, promoting technology and other good things of this world are concerned, commerce, business and capitalism are okay. We need these, for example, so we can get the libraries at universities, art centers throughout the world, and charitable giving of other kinds. But this is all merely of instrumental significance and cannot be credited morally. So people in business cannot feel moral pride in what they do – instead they must do *pro bono* work, be socially responsible, and serve not the investors and owners but the stakeholders in their enterprise (neighborhoods, parks, schools, churches and such). Take Bill Gates and Warren Buffet as cases in point.

No educator is asked to earn moral credit via socially responsible works – being an educator is honorable enough, in and of itself. Artists are praised for their visions – never mind that these are often pretty egotistical, and self-expressive with little or no benefit to anyone but the artist who flourishes through the creative process. But those in business are most often disparaged, and the reason is that they cannot pretend to anyone that they are serving the muse or seeking to elevate the lives of the young, or doing other high-minded things. All they are after is supposedly the bottom line, never mind that the bottom line is but a kind of liberty, spread around for people to pursue their own goals and not have to beg for some share of the common wealth.

The main problem, in short, is that capitalism is unabashedly worldly, tied to how well we – each of us individually, as part of the natural world – might do; indeed, how well off we are as natural beings with tastes, preferences, desires, likes and wants. All this is deemed to be not cool!

Why, in contrast to people in business, are environmentalists managing to come off so holier-than-thou? They really do not do much, other than protest and ask for more power to stop the rest of us from doing what they deem is unimportant or harmful to nature. It's because they can give out the word that they care not for humanity but for something greater, Nature or, in some cases, the plans of the creator. They preach that we must be stewards or wardens – caretakers – but not owners or proprietors of what there is in nature surrounding us. They can insist on their moral superiority because, well, they are unselfish, good not even to other people but only to other non-people – for example, endangered animal species! This, misanthrope, is the *reductio ad absurdum* of the altruist morality that has been so influential and has made it so fashionable to denigrate whatever serves to do us good, right here and now. That damnable bottom line, that rotten private interest, that me, me and more me – namely, a human individual!

Well, commerce, business and capitalism will not get a fair shake unless this nonsense is given up and rethought very carefully and critically, indeed. It is time to credit them for what they are good for, namely, ourselves. Somehow, oddly, there seems to be nothing wrong with medicine, nutrition, psychiatry, or exercise, all of which unabashedly serve us well. It seems these professions can disguise themselves as aiming for something idealistically noble and superior, even though that is just misguided. Their nobility consists of serving us well, here on Earth!

Business must be shown to do nothing less, and shown to do it in spades and to its total credit. After that, the appeal of socialism, communism, and even the welfare state will have some serious competition. But not before.

Chapter 4

TAXES AND GOVERNMENT

1.   A TAX GLITCH

In the last analysis, taxes are a relic of feudal rule, where society is composed of subjects, not sovereign citizens. Taxes are what these subjects pay for the privilege of being a monarch's wards, given that the king owns – which in this case means forcibly possesses – everything.

But many of the features of monarchies retained a life of their own even after monarchies were abolished or at least diminished to ceremonial status. Taxation is one such institution. It should eventually be replaced with a system of fees for service rendered.[22] And in the USA there is implicit awareness of this when it is argued that, ultimately, taxes are paid voluntarily. It is a fiction, but one required by the logic of the inalienability of individual rights to life, liberty and the pursuit of happiness (or property).

How would such a system work? It would involve, mainly, attaching a fee to all contracts drawn up among citizens, contracts that require the force of law for their backing – including courts, police, military, etc., all of which serve the purpose of keeping the peace, including securing a civilized adjudication of contractual disputes. One would still be free to enter into agreements apart from contracts, via a handshake or a promise. (Quite possibly, although these are enforceable in some courts today, in a tax-free system non-user-fee payers would not have recourse to the courts.) But the millions of corporations doing business cannot afford such trust, so they would enter into contractual relationships, and would need to pay for the service governments provide to back these up.

No, this system isn't around the corner, although it ought to be. What we have instead is the continuation of the monarchical practice of legalized extortion. It is a corrupt system – but corruption can be greater or smaller, so it is worth looking at some taxes to see how desperate government is to dip into everything citizens own and enjoy.

---

[22]Citizenship, of course, is not costless and requires of citizens some services, such as testifying in criminal trials where their testimony is crucial for achieving justice, via the subpoena process. Yet when justice may be served without requiring such services, that is how it must be served lest it undermine its very purpose, namely, the full and consistent securing of our fundamental, unalienable rights.

A good example is the taxing of tips.

In the state of Nevada, there was a debate recently about this issue, though in some other states, including California, the issue is by now moot. Should the tips paid to those working in restaurants, especially, but in many other lines of work – furniture deliverers, for example, or barbers – be taxed?

Government officials have been claiming that tips should be taxed because they are a form of income. But are they really?

Consider that income is payment for services rendered. If you do not pay the income of those who work in restaurants – for example, if you walk out without paying for your dinner – you are subject to prosecution. If you don't pay for the furniture delivered to your home, you can be sued. If your barber does not receive the payment you owe for the haircut he or she provides, again you are in trouble with the law.

But now ask yourself – as per the suggestion of my good friend. Jackson R. Wheeler, who called this point to my attention – if you don't pay a tip, what happens? Nothing much, other than getting some people angry at you. But angry or not, no legal action can be taken against you, because you haven't failed to pay for the service rendered. You simply didn't provide a customary gift to those who rendered the service – a gift, granted, that is almost automatic, but a gift, nevertheless.

Gifts are not taxable, certainly not as income. Yet in California, for example, restaurants must add 8% of their income to the income they earn, as an estimate of the tips received. It is ridiculous but not surprising. The government wants whatever it can get, and unless you – meaning the people of the political sphere – are legally, constitutionally savvy, you will get rooked.

Just goes to show you – extortionists never get enough.

2.   GOVERNMENT BUDGET CRISES

Budget crises – at all levels of government – are routine, these days. Although there may be one or two years of surpluses, in most regions they are followed by many years of deficits. If governments were judged by the standards of private firms, most of them would be bankrupt. However, because they can use the tax collector to obtain funds or, in the case of the federal governments of most countries, print money, governments are nearly immune to the serious adverse consequences of financial mismanagement.

Why do governments get into such scrapes so often? It isn't out-and-out corruption, except rarely. The problem is systemic.

There is serious work afoot, now, that answers this question. Essentially, governments lack the needed basis for assessing the relationship between their resources and their expenses. They are unavoidably ill-informed because the means by which that relationship is best understood is plainly unavailable to governments.

3. THE CALCULATION PROBLEM

Ludwig von Mises, the leading economist of the "Austrian School," established as long ago as 1922[23] that, for there to be meaningful and useful economic calculation, there must be a free-market place where people – for whom governments work – can allocate their resources for whatever they deem worthwhile. When they do this, their millions of purchasing instances communicates to producers in the marketplace what is in demand, what customers will buy, as well as what they will leave sitting on the shelves. This information is vital for producers to be able to estimate what they need to do, and how much of what is likely to sell. Inventories, therefore, will be adjusted very closely to what people who shop are likely to purchase.

The system that best communicates this information between buyers and sellers is capitalism. What makes that possible is that people in a capitalist system have a reasonably clear idea of what belongs to them, through the institution of private property rights. So, they know what they can spend and what would break their budgets. Even buying on credit is adjusted to their capacity to carry debt. Therefore, they have a very clear signal to warn them about overspending.

When an economic system has this advantage, it is less likely to experience major vacillations, including financial crises, because, on average, people will balance their economic purchases with their available resources. When you put that in terms of several hundred million transactions in the marketplace, a very complicated yet smoothly functioning system results.[24]

Von Mises, and his most famous student, Nobel Laureate F. A. Hayek, presented these ideas in the great debate about whether socialist economies can function.[25] As one of the most famous American (Marxist) socialist economists put it recently, "... Ludwig von Mises ... had written of the 'impossibility' of socialism, arguing that no Central Planning Board could ever gather

---

[23]Ludwig von Mises, *Socialism; an economic and sociological analysis*; translated by J. Kahane (London: Jonathan J. Cape, 1936).

[24]The idea that capitalism created the Great Depression and other market upheavals is a dangerous myth, as the works of Milton Friedman and Anna Schwartz, *Great Contraction, 1929–1933* (Chicago: University of Chicago Press, 1962) and others have shown.

[25]F. A. Hayek, ed., *Collectivist economic planning: critical studies on the possibilities of socialism* [with essays by N.G. Pierson, Ludwig von Mises, Georg Halm, and Erico Barone] (London: George Routledge & Sons, 1938).

the enormous amount of information needed to create a workable economic system... It turns out, of course, that Mises was right ..."[26]

That admission by Heilbroner came, however, only after the collapse of Soviet-style socialism. And the fact that the point applies also to welfare states – systems of government where the state assumes many production and distribution functions that, under capitalism, would remain in the private sector – was not noticed even by those who saw its relevance to socialist systems. Yet von Mises himself, and many of his students, realized that any attempt at top-down calculation of economic relations is going to be futile. Governments have no ability to gauge what they need and what they must deliver, especially not when it comes to such essentially private goods and services as insurance, housing, medical care, transportation, schooling and the like.[27] Whatever reasons might be given for why governments ought to provide such goods and services, there is one that will never be convincing, namely, that they will deal with the economic issues successfully. They just cannot.

The reason is relatively simple: When you deal with funds that aren't yours, which you collect at gun point from others, you never really know what there is for you to spend and on what you should spend it. This is, essentially, both an economic and a moral problem. Those who do not own the resources simply have no clear way to know what they ought to do with those resources, even when they are in their legal possession.

4.   "PUBLIC CHOICE" OBSTACLES

Another group of economists, lead by Nobel Laureate Jim Buchanan and his colleague Gordon Tullock at George Mason University, produced public choice theory. The purpose of this theory is to gain a clear understanding of the economic elements of government bureaucracies. Buchanan and Tullock argued[28] that bureaucrats are not unlike agents in a capitalist market place, so they seek to advance their economic objectives. However, because they do not have the feedback mechanism of the market, nor the budget constraints of market agents, their "profit maximization" procedures are far more unruly than are those of private market agents. Accordingly, government bureaucracies are nearly always mismanaged. People always spend more than they have, lacking the natural constraints that most of us face as we go shopping.

---

[26]Robert Heilbroner, "After Communism," *The New Yorker* (September 10, 1990), p. 92.

[27]Arguably, when it comes to essentially public goods and services such as military defense, police protection and judicial services, government can assess cost and benefits. See, Tibor R. Machan, *Private Rights and Public Illusions* (New Brunswick, NJ: Transaction Books, 1995).

[28]Op. cit., Buchanan and Tullock, *The Calculus of Consent*.

5. SOME CONCRETE CASES IN POINT

Perhaps both of these theories will leave many wondering just what in particular they identify in day-to-day, real-life circumstances. Some examples will help to answer this.

When I was in the US Air Force, I worked as a civil engineering draftsman. After Christmas each year, I suddenly had to work overtime. There was no increase of workload – most people just sat around during the day but then went to work from 6–9 PM, when the overtime would have to be put in. As a soldier, I didn't receive overtime pay but the engineering staff, comprised of government employees, did. Upon inquiring why the overtime was necessary, a G-14 explained that they all needed the overtime income so as to pay for their Christmas purchases.

Another case will help illustrate how the theories sketched above play out in practice. Each time a new budget had to be submitted, suddenly several rush jobs had to be done, such as building a little flower garden by the main gate. It was never anything very important. Upon inquiry, it turned out that we needed to spend all the money in our budget so that we could ask for more money for the next fiscal period.

Yet another occasion helps us see the way public choice theory, specifically, manifests itself. As a member of a Department of Education panel that developed and administered a fellowship program in Washington, I saw the application of the theory. After two years of going through all the work to set it up and get it off the ground, some of the panelists decided they wanted to apply to Congress for more money for this program. Why? They wanted to do it better and get more things done with it. When it was pointed out that this wasn't really our job, few of them cared. (The only thing that prevented the request from being sent to Congress is that, the day we met to consider the idea, the Nobel committee in Sweden announced the Prize for Jim Buchanan, and I explained to everyone what occasioned the event: namely, the development of public choice theory, a theory that explained so clearly why people are trying to get more money from Congress for this project.[29])

When the issue of state fiscal mismanagement comes up, many look for bits and pieces of evidence of wrong-doing and even corruption. But that is not what makes sense of this recurrent phenomenon. It is the fact that governments, as a rule, are very bad at economic calculation.[30] They are ill-composed

---

[29]This occurred in October of 1985, in Washington, D.C., at the meeting of the Jacob J. Javits Graduate Fellowship Program meeting.

[30]Yet another theory bears on this issue, also the product of the work of a Nobel Laureate in economics. See Kenneth J. Arrow, *Social Choice and Individual Values* (New York: John Wiley, 1963). Arrow shows that the ranking of collective or social priorities is impossible in de-

for that purpose. All the incentives are wrong, and there are no constraints that guide people to be rational about how to spend the resources.

This is why so many countries around the globe are experimenting with privatization – which is the shifting of many kinds of responsibilities from the public to the private sector.

6.   GOVERNMENT REGULATION VS. THE FREE SOCIETY[31]

Over the years, I have been persistent in my criticism of petty tyrannies such as government regulation of business, government licensing of professions, and so on.[32] My central objection is that they all involve prior restraint, a coercive intervention in people's conduct that does not have anything to do with defending individual rights, the only goal that justifies the use of force in human affairs.

Very recently, and finally, someone in mainstream circles has chosen to address my argument. Edward Soule, of Georgetown University's McDonough School of Business, wrote a book, *Morality & Markets, The Ethics of Government Regulation*, in which he spends some time addressing the essentially libertarian, natural-rights case I have made against this widespread practice. It is a very respectful, civilized criticism, the tone of which is unobjectionable. Given that the position I have defended is quite radical (some would even call it extreme), I am very pleased that someone of as much distinction as Soule has decided to address it.

Let me now get to the substance of Soule's critique. First of all, he disputes the libertarian argument against regulation which I put forth by claiming that, if it were consistently applied, such a very practical institution as central banking would have to be abolished. As he puts it,

> "According to these [Machan's libertarian] criteria, central bank activity is an example of unjustified regulation because it affects the value of privately held funds. And a theory that disqualifies the legitimacy of one of the primary institutions of economic organization has some explaining to do. Specifically, it must explain why nominal property rights are more important than the stabilizing effects of

---

mocratic societies. That, too, contributes to fiscal mismanagement and, of course, everyone's dissatisfaction with what government does.

[31] This discussion was previously published in *Business and Professional Ethics Journal*, Vol. 22, No. 1 (2004), pp. 77–83.

[32] My first efforts were included in Tibor R. Machan and M. Bruce Johnson, eds., *Rights and Regulation* (San Francisco: Pacific Institute for Policy Studies, 1983). See "The Petty Tyranny of Government Regulation," pp. 259–288. Later I wrote *Private Rights and Public Illusions* (New Brunswick, NJ: Transaction Books, 1995) in which I develop the criticism in much greater detail. Soule considers only the earlier essay.

central banks and their ability to ameliorate the risk of a monetary crisis inflicting damage on the real economy."[33]

There is more, but let me address the above immediately so it will not detain us very long. To start with, central banking activity does not merely affect the value of privately held funds. Although my argument isn't based on such consequences of government regulation, it bears mentioning that central banking activity has an impact on the conduct of investors, savers, and various other business professionals who are, among other things, shut out of competition with the central banks, who may not lend at various rates because of what the central bank decides, etc.

The next point to be made is that the claim that property rights are nominal is entirely ad hoc, in this comment. Certainly the criticism I deploy rejects that assumption. When I own funds that I must use within certain limits that the central bank decides, my property rights are impeded, and this is no mere conventional matter, any more than it would be a mere matter if some burglar robbed me of household goods which I came by justly. One might ask, when denying the burglar's authority to commit the robbery, "Why should mere nominal property rights trump his quite possibly urgent pursuit of certain goals, such as feeding his children or taking a long-deserved vacation?"

Still remaining with the quoted passage, there is no support given anywhere by Soule for the crucial claim that "central banks [have the] ability to ameliorate the risk of a monetary crisis inflicting damage on the real economy." That such a claim requires support and not mere assertion may not be evident to someone who rejects libertarian analyses of political economy. Yet even as widely recognized an authority on central banks as Alan Greenspan has argued that, at best, central banks are superfluous, and at their worst they are destructive of stability in the real economy.[34]

---

[33]Edward Soule, *Markets & Morality, The Ethics of Government Regulation* (Lanham, MD: Rowman & Littlefield, 2003), p. 81.

[34]Alan Greenspan, "The Evolution of Banking in A Market Economy," *Journal of Private Enterprise*, Vol. XIII (1997), pp. 195–203. The following is most indicative of Greenspan's views for central banking:

> When the efforts of the Federal Reserve failed to prevent the bank collapses of the 1930s, the Banking Act of 1933 created federal deposit insurance. The subsequent evidence appears persuasive that the combination of a lender of last resort (the Federal Reserve) and federal deposit insurance has contributed significantly to financial stability and has accordingly achieved wide support within the Congress. Inevitably, however, such significant government intervention has not been an unmixed blessing. The federal safety net for banks clearly has diminished the effectiveness of private market regulation and created perverse incentives in the banking system. To cite the most obvious and painful example, without federal deposit insurance, private markets presumably would never have permitted thrift institutions

Libertarians have argued for decades that it was the activity of the U. S. Federal Reserve Bank that produced the crucial causes of the Great Depression, contrary to what mainstream political economics teaches.[35] Greenspan backed up this claim with a fairly detailed history of American banking. Judging by his analysis, the only reason any government regulation has been introduced is that politicians reacted with panic to certain factors that had an impact on the financial markets, factors that government regulators couldn't ever anticipate or prevent. And once politicians introduced government regulation, it had two results: (a) they displaced well-working non-government regulation and (b) they produced failures in the regulated marketplace, which politicians then tried to remedy with further government regulation.

While supporters of free markets are well aware of this history of government regulation nearly everywhere – panic met with political reaction, which then creates serious problems to which politicians again react with more of their interference, ultimately leading to a less and less free market that has all kinds of negative consequences which are explained, perversely enough, by the alleged inadequacies of the free market – the general public, as well as much of academia, are uninformed about this pattern. Many historians of business continue to make it appear that government regulation had been introduced on various fronts because a *bona fide* free market produced very undesirable economic results – because of genuine market failures, that is. Thus, from elementary to graduate schools, historians and political scientists keep spreading the myth that it is because of laissez-faire that America had its Great Depression. It is wrong but it is taught to students everywhere. And Soule is a good example of someone who fits this characterization, accepting without question, or even the need of a footnote, his claim that free markets without central banks produce economic instability which central banks can prevent.

Soule goes on to criticize the view that the prior restraint in government regulation is akin to prior restraint in the criminal law. As he puts it,

---

to purchase the portfolios that brought down the industry insurance fund and left future generations of taxpayers responsible for huge losses . . . .(p. 202)

[35] See, for example, Murray N. Rothbard, *America's Great Depression* (Princeton, NJ: Van Nostrand, 1963), Milton Friedman and Anna Jacobson Schwartz, *The great contraction, 1929–1933*, 1st ed. (Princeton, N.J., Princeton University Press, 1965), Gene Smiley, *Rethinking the Great Depression* (Chicago: I. R. Dee, 2002), and Jim Powell, *FDR's Folly* (New York : Crown Forum, 2003). Citing these works and quoting Alan Greenspan's remarks earlier will not suffice to prove the point advanced by these authors, nor my own *opposition* to government regulation. What it will show is that Soule fails even to acknowledge widely available sources of argument challenging a premise in his *defense* of government regulation, namely, that the U.S. federal reserve system, and central banking in general, are morally preferable to an unregulated financial market.

"Criminal law and statutory regulation are similar insofar as they impinge on rights by restricting the range of options available. That is, they forbid some choices under threat of punishment. But the fact that they do so in advance of an actual harm is not necessarily morally right or wrong; it depends upon the option that is being foreclosed. More specifically, in the case of commercial regulation, it depends upon whether the option was one that individuals or firms were morally obliged to avoid in the first place."[36]

Contrary to Soule's claim, however, criminal law could also preemptively restrict conduct on the grounds that such conduct could only lead to something bad and untoward – as when it would arrest people who seemed predisposed (for example, genetically) to do something wrong but hadn't yet done so. The government could require the supervision of such persons, making it impossible for them to act badly. That is what statutory regulations do: they direct individuals and firms to act prudently, when they might not but could very well do so.

The main reason why this – and preemptive intervention – is wrong, contrary to Soule's claim, is that it removes moral agency by mandating the agent's conduct, even when the agent might have done the right thing on his own initiative. A citizen in any profession who is barred from having the choice between doing what is right versus what is wrong is not capable of acting rightly (or wrongly, of course) as a moral agent but is coercively made to behave as the regulators deem proper. But then the actions lack moral significance.[37]

Soule claims, for example, that: "The commercial carrier that must comply with safety rules has not lost anything in terms of its legitimate aspirations to be free."[38] Nothing except, of course, a portion of his or her freedom to be a moral agent. It is this loss of liberty, the most important element of personhood in a just society, that government regulations – from censorship and drug prohibition to licensing and business regulations – rule out.[39] The individuals

---

[36] Soule, op. cit., p. 83.

[37] For a development of this point, see Douglas J. Den Uyl, "Freedom and Virtue," *Reason Papers* (Winter, 1979), Tibor R. Machan, "Ethics vs. Coercion: Morality or Just Values?" in Llewellyn H. Rockwell, Jr., et al., ed., *Man, Economy and Liberty* (Auburn, AL: Ludwig von Mises Institute, 1988), and "Liberty & Morality," *Think*, Issue 9 (Spring 2005), 87–89.

[38] Ibid.

[39] Not all professions in the USA are government-regulated or -licensed. For example, journalists and ministers are protected by the First Amendment to the US Constitution. This, of course, is arguably a rank injustice. Why should journalist and ministers be exempt from government meddling when the rest of us suffer their intervention on so many fronts? There really is no good reason for such favoritism. Why should the criminal law, especially when it comes to journalistic conduct, observe the ban on prior restraint and other violations of due process while professionals are being regimented – subjected to various rules and fined if they do not comply – by governments, despite having done nothing (nor, indeed, having been suspected of having done anything) wrong at all?

and the firms they comprise will not be in a position to choose to do what is right because they are coerced to behave as the government requires them to behave.[40]

It is, not so incidentally, also quite naïve to believe that government regulations routinely promote good behavior. Many are drafted so as to serve special interests or to favor certain constituencies over others, and so it is wrong to think, as Soule seems to, that government regulations somehow guarantee even good behavior, let alone encourage morally proper conduct.[41]

The challenges Soule advances against my criticism of government regulation are not insignificant. However, they can, I believe, be met.

I should make clear, in conclusion, that what I say on this topic is motivated by the more general view that the right to individual liberty – including the right to private property – is fundamental and based on human nature, not on convention (although convention or, rather, contextual elaboration, plays a part in the development in the law of this right), and is indivisible. Even more generally put, the idea is that free adult men and women are more likely to produce both justice and welfare than will, as a rule, even slightly regimented ones.

It may be worth noting that some folks who agree that government regulation is largely wrong – at least inefficient – hold that in some cases it is inescapable. The example is air or water pollution. Yet it is arguable that, in such cases, what is needed isn't prior restraint but a sound system of tort law applied to some people who are imposing personal or property injuries on others. It seems to me highly desirable to avoid sanctioning any type of government precautionary rules in the market place, since such rules establish a bad precedent and punish many innocent people, in any case.[42]

---

[40]This same problem afflicts anti-discrimination laws. The way to deal with racism and sexism is not via what amounts to a kind of prior restraint but by way of disclosure laws. To wit, unless it is made clear, up front, that an establishment uses discriminatory policies in hiring, selling, subcontracting and the like, the common law will be available to impose serious costs and penalties for ad hoc discrimination. But such discrimination, if fully disclosed, must not be banned in a free society. For more on this, see Tibor R. Machan and James E. Chesher, *A Primer on Business Ethics* (Lanham, MD: Rowman & Littlefield, 2002).

[41]The view that government regulators are captured by the industries they are supposed to regulate has been advanced not only by libertarian economists but also by economic democrats such as Ralph Nader. See, Sam Peltzman, *Political participation and government regulation*, (Chicago: University of Chicago Press, 1998). And see Robert C. Fellmeth, *The interstate commerce comission, the public interest and the ICC; The Ralph Nader study group report on the Interstate Commerce Commission and transportation* (New York, Grossman Publishers, 1970).

[42]For more on this, see Tibor R. Machan, *Private Rights and Public Illusions* (Oakland, CA: The Independent Institute; New Brunswick, NJ: Transaction Books, 1995), especially "Pollution and Political Theory."

7. LIBERTY V. COERCION: THE BURDEN OF PROOF

When I become aware of some new means by which some of my fellow citizens aim to encroach upon other people's liberty, I tend to oppose such measures. Some time ago, a local television editorial advocated the establishment of a new Federal agency to protect the interests of consumers. Later, I discussed this with some acquaintances. When they heard my protests, they immediately raised their eyebrows. "Why not?" they asked. "Why should the government stay out of the business of protecting the consumer?"

I tried to explain, starting from the principle of *caveat emptor* and going on to the impossibility of protecting consumers against their would-be protectors. I even argued for some alternative system, such as an insurance program, whereby the consumer can protect himself without involving everyone in this mission.

None of this seemed to help my case. At each turn, I was simply told, "Well, such an agency might still help; it might be able to do something to avoid difficulties with business firms that make shoddy products and cause all sorts of trouble for the consumer." And in a way this is right; such an agency might very well do some good for somebody. But this seemed hardly sufficient to justify its establishment.

Each time I emerge from such a discussion, I make several resolutions. Most frequently I resolve that it does little good to talk about such matters in brief encounters – hardly anyone is prepared to investigate the issues carefully enough to learn anything. It seems inconceivable to most people that agencies of the government should not get involved with such activities as consumer protection, that is, protecting people against their own carelessness. This, despite what Herbert Spencer discovered some time ago: "The ultimate result of shielding men from the effects of folly is to fill the world with fools." It becomes evident in these discussions that people nowadays rarely think in terms of principles. Who wants to apply an old-fashioned principle to a modern practice? Regulating business firms seems, to many people, to be light-years away from regulating the work of newspaper and television writers; consumer protection and censorship are thought to have nothing to do with each other. Finally, there is always a problem in protesting some new infringement on human liberty, because so many exist already. What point is there in protesting at this juncture? After all, we live with so much coercion and force already! Thus, the matter is purely academic, or so these people seem to believe.

8.   FOR A BETTER WAY

How, then, does one combat this prevailing tendency to run to government in the hope of achieving every goal that seems desirable? "Why not?" "It might work, despite the record of failures." Let me share some of my thoughts on the matter.

When a program is advocated by someone, others are entitled to know his reason if the program involves them in some unavoidable manner. If I decide tomorrow that I will try, from now on, to help America's consumers by writing letters to business executives, accompanying buyers on their trips to the store, publishing books about the quality and variety of products available, or the like, no one else need be worried about why I am doing this. I may be someone with benevolent motives, a guilt complex, or a plan to strike it rich through a consumer-protection business. Other people are free to ignore my efforts, or to join in them if they so choose. But they have no right to demand that I furnish them with a justification for my actions. (They could conclude, even rightly, that I am wasting my time, that I will go broke, or something of that sort – just as they could judge my plans to be very valuable. But they cannot justifiably demand that I account to them as to why I am embarking on my mission.)

The case is different when my plans must necessarily involve others. Take, for example, the editorial which urged the creation of a Federal consumer-protection agency. Others will be involved – including taxpayers, business employees who must comply with regulations, and so on. At this juncture, it seems reasonable to demand that proponents of such a scheme fully explain and justify why other persons should be involved and obliged to join in their mission.

But this is not as simple a demand as it seems. There are times that we believe, without the slightest doubt, that we are entitled to something; and when it is not delivered, we believe we may take measures to remedy the situation. There is no wide-scale agreement on such matters; people differ drastically as to what each believes to be his rights. One person believes that he is entitled to some help with his medical problems whenever he cannot handle them, whereas another may believe that he alone is responsible for such matters as his health, welfare and education. To the first person, it will seem self-evident that others ought to help with his troubles, whether or not they choose to do so; he would think it our natural duty, an obligation we have toward each other, the performance of which must, at times, be enforced lest his needs be neglected. The second person, however, would consider the duties we have toward each other to be an outgrowth of our own choices; even if some of us have natural obligations toward others, we ought not to be forced to perform them. Indeed, if force were to be justifiably utilized, it would be to see that we are left free to lead our own lives and to be charitable in our own way. There needs to be a philosophical justification of the limits we ought to draw around our actions, to help identify what we are entitled to do, and what range of actions we can perform without limiting the liberty of others. This in turn might help explain why we would demand justification before we would allow another to involve us in his schemes. The person who believes that his medical problems should be alleviated through help from others may so believe in all honesty and sincerity. If so, at least he may be invited to consider a philosophical system under which various claims might be justified. Perhaps then he will see that, to get the help he wants, he must justify his claim that we should give it to him and also justify any force he would use toward that end.

9. SINCERITY OF PURPOSE

But such a philosophical theory is not a simple matter to develop. Nor can it be communicated in discussion of such an isolated issue as a Federal consumer-protection agency. Such discussion will likely get nowhere unless the parties have the sincerity of purpose, time, and knowledge to cover the entire range of related ideas, back to the theory of liberty.

Some have sought to shorten the discussion, saying that each individual's person or body sets the limit of other people's authority. But clearly this will not suffice, for it does not cover such things as our house, books, automobile, or musical composition. The theory must relate all such properties to us in some way that will justify our keeping them for ourselves if we so choose. Opponents of liberty notoriously complain that Americans have stolen their present land holdings from the Indians. And if this is so, do we have any defense against those who would steal from us, in turn, these lands and their fruits? Do thieves or recipients of stolen goods have any justifiable complaint if the goods are stolen again?

Even with a sound theory of property rights, the argument for liberty may be lost in the mists of democracy. How often we hear that living in a democracy involves giving up certain rights to privacy, property, and the like. And if that be so, may the individual logically claim anything at all that is not allowed by the majority – or its representatives? What, in short, justifies the view that the exercise of majority rule is limited by certain principles defining human liberty – certain inalienable, universal, and absolute human rights?

So what is one to do in the face of such widely entrenched coercion and political intervention? It seems that education in broad political principles and their philosophical justification must be the general approach. If there is a reasonable case for such coercive intervention, let the burden of proof be on those who are proposing it. Let them try to justify coercion, even in one or two isolated cases. Let them 'prove' to our satisfaction why, e.g., consumer protection justifies that millions of others will be deprived of their income without their consent. Let them try to demonstrate the virtue of coercion, for they are the ones who are embarking on the course of action that will necessarily involve the lives of others.

Without a demonstration of the validity of the explicit or implicit claim that others should be forced to comply with the aggressor's plans – however noble these may be – we are entitled to treat his proposal as something entirely arbitrary, without support in truth and justice.

Nor is all this merely an academic exercise. When they are thus challenged, amazingly little attempted justification is forthcoming from most of those who insist that coercion is a valid means for solving human problems. They simply hadn't thought about it that way. And such a provocative challenge may well be their first short lesson toward an education in the nature of human liberty.

10.   POWER & LIBERTY

When the case for human liberty was initially made, it was without benefit of a sound moral argument, mostly by reliance on a value-free framework. The one quasi-moral promise made on behalf of the system was that it would promote the diminution of political power. Freedom would put everyone on a politically equal footing, since governments should serve us all by protecting our right to liberty. Yes, these were moral terms but heavily mixed with the conceptual machinery of mechanistic physics. Even Adam Smith's idea of "natural liberty" functioned mostly to indicate the absence of impediments to self-interestedly motivated behavior, not as a normative political concept.

In our day, too, many people champion liberal societies on the grounds that the power of governments is limited, restricted, minimized, and so forth. As Robert Nisbet puts it, "liberalism ... is historically a theory of immunity from power ..."[43] And within this school of liberalism, economic power is not regarded to be of anything but productive significance – a rising tide of economic prosperity lifts all ships, and so forth.

Critics of liberalism have never quite bought this line of defense. Marx, for example, made clear that "This kind of liberty [the free competition of liberal societies] is thus at the same time the most complete suppression of all individual liberty and total subjugation of individuality to social conditions which take the form of material forces – and even of all-powerful objects that are independent of the individuals relating to them."[44]

---

[43] Robert Nisbet, "The Contexts of Democracy," *Presidential Essay* (Washington, DC: The Heritage Foundation, 2003), p. 15.

[44] Karl Marx, *Grundrisse* (New York: Harper & Row, 1970), p. 131.

Marx's point was that not only is the legal framework of capitalist societies – contract and property laws – a form of power and control over the lives of citizens, but these give rise to such massive features as technological instruments – factories, dams, highways, ships, and so forth – which exert a great deal of influence over people's lives. So, for the critics, the difference between liberal and non-liberal societies and their economic systems consists of *who* has power, not whether power is exercised. A simple example will make this point clear.

In a free market, the labor contract is usually drawn up in such a way that, in principle, both the owner and employee of a firm have the power to terminate the employment relationship. Yet, because of the durable economic importance of capital under the free market system, the employer's power is referred to in some of the literature on political economy as "employment at will" (of the employer).

So, while government does not have the power to impose employment terms on the labor relationship, it is claimed that the firm largely does. (Actually, if there's a competitive employment market, this is clearly false.) State power is limited in a free country; the power of firms, that is, those who legally own the property that can be improved by hired labor, is plenty extensive. For our purposes, we may ignore here that employee associations, unions and the like, as well as certain kind of employees, do have immense economic power, as well. Consider famous movie actors, baseball or basketball players, even star academics – they are in many cases able to set the terms of their employment, nearly unopposed by their employers. We may ignore this here because all that these cases prove is that *both employees and employers* do in fact possess economic power in the free market, not that the free markets are immune to power. (They may, of course, be *de jure* immune to certain types of power, such as outright physical violence.)

Indeed, for critics of classic liberalism, this power is more insidious because, they argue, the power of the state could be exercised rationally, while that of the unruly property owners cannot be. As Marx puts it in the next sentence, "The only rational answer to the deification of free competition by the middle-class prophets, or its diapolisation by the socialists, lies in its own development."[45] That development, of course, will lead to the abolition of capitalism and the emergence of socialism.

How can one answer this line of criticism without some recourse to values or moral judgment? It is not possible. In free markets, economic power is often unequally allocated, distributed by the choices of market agents. Is the distribution that results – the greater power base of economically successful persons – justifiable?

---

[45] *Ibid.*

To put the point bluntly, the only way to adjudicate this dispute is by determining whether the power of the state versus that which property owners will exercise is morally or politically justified. In other words, should government or the property owner have the authority to exercise power?

It is futile to deny that owners have and exercise considerable economic power. Such power is the ability to make what one wants actually happen. When a worker wants to keep a job but the owner does not want to employ him or her, the worker loses out, usually, although on a larger scale this doesn't hold true. Of course, if the worker wants to quit, he or she will win, but that is often the less *visible* situation. Just consider the worry about downsizing. It is also often true that employers are able to find replacements for workers more readily than workers can find new jobs on their own terms. Even when this is not the case, the worker's situation is deemed to be more dire because of the often greater wealth of the employer. Whether this imbalance of bargaining power is justified or not is what ultimately must be addressed by those who believe that there is greater merit in a free market system than in one that is regimented by government – say, via a workers' democracy.

Does the property owner or employer have the proper, rightful authority to exercise the greater economic power, or ought it to belong to the worker (or the government acting on behalf of the worker)? Is it justified for workers to invoke the force of government to back up their authority, thus balancing power?

This is where a theory of property rights and the authority of government to protect these rights enters the picture of political economy. If a firm is rightfully, properly owned by the legal owners, and if the law of property and the resulting institution and enforcement of contract law are just, then the firm's power is not arbitrary or unjust, even though it is engaged in the wielding of power – which it may also misuse at times by, for example, firing people it should not, based on the standard of professional contribution to the firm's tasks. (To claim that this never happens is inaccurate – some employers are misguided in what they want from employees, just as some employees are in what they want from employers.)

If, however, the law of property of liberal-capitalist societies is wrong, so that the workers de facto own the firm (because, say, their labor built it up), not those who in such societies *de jure* do, then the critics of (classical) liberalism, especially socialists, are right.

The issue is crucial. And liberalism needs theoretically to extend itself into this area of moral and political philosophy, in order to give its political-economic system a chance.

The practical results, too, would be immense. If it could be shown to workers and all (including their intellectual guardians) – who are rational and can deal with the assessment of theories – that the legal owners rightfully own their property in liberal-capitalist systems, their protest would dissipate.

Consider that many of those not obviously involved in capitalist endeavors, but who nevertheless clearly benefit economically from their creative achievements, such as artists and scientists, have little difficulty in exercising the power they have over their creations (as when they set terms of trade in trading copyrights). When a Woody Allen protests that his films ought not to be colorized because, well, he does not want them to be, this is deemed to be perfectly okay, since it is, after all, *his* art that is at stake. Never mind that the broadcasters who would colorize them – and the public who apparently prefers color movies to black-and-white ones – want something else. They lack the justification to have their will realized.

It is perhaps a little less easy to tell why a beautiful woman should have full authority over the benefits gained from her beauty, given that this beauty is not mostly her achievement. Yet neither is it anyone else's, just as the better heart or liver or general health of someone, from which one can definitely benefit a good deal – in contrast to the loss of those lacking it – belongs to those who possess it, never mind whether they earned it.

Still, free market champions need to demonstrate that such benefits are *rightfully* owned by those who in law have or want title to them.

The point here isn't to spell out the answer to why classical liberal-capitalist ownership rights are justified. To just hint at this, its justification is akin to that of the justification of a woman's claim to govern the use of her body, even if it (a) is a much-desired body by many over whom she, therefore, has and can exercise some measure of power, and (b) is not really fully her achievement to have the body she may have. (I intend nothing dualistic by the use of these terms. Also, in the USA and in many other legal systems, women now often lack the power to, say, benefit from their good looks since they may not be employed on that basis, only on the basis of what is deemed to be politically correct, e.g., their skills.)

The point is merely to indicate that, without such a justification, relying solely on the greater or lesser exercise of power within different systems, the case for freedom cannot be made.

All systems of political economy witness the exercise of power. The question is, in which system is such power exercised with greater moral authority? If I am the producer or owner of the wealth with which I make an impact on society, then others who can feel this impact have no basis for complaint. If the talents I am born with, or the genetic composition, are indeed mine to use as I judge suitable, then the power I exert by this use is politically justified, even if not always necessarily morally wise. Am I like the influential novelist or painter whose reputation is earned, based on effort, talent and opportunity, even if it does give the author a greater role in shaping society than those possess who have produced or created less? If the author cannot be credited with and deemed to be the rightful owner of what he or she has done, then his or her greater role in shaping society is undeserved and others can bellyache about it endlessly. To whom should such power belong, then, given that it will be a factor in any system?

Chapter 5

ADVERTISING, PROPAGANDA AND JOURNALISM

1. WHY IS THE ETHICS OF ADVERTISING IMPORTANT?

When we try to judge an activity or institution, we need to know its nature and purpose. If you travel, you need to know where you want to go in order to tell how well you are progressing. If one wishes to judge parenting or teaching or scholarship, one needs to know what these are, so as to determine whether a given instance fulfills its nature, function or purpose – that is, whether it is a good instance of its kind.

Unless we know what advertising is, we cannot judge or evaluate it or what others claim about it. One might think here of what is involved in malpractice lawsuits. Malpractice presupposes standards of conduct. Without standards, there can be no way to identify and distinguish what is and is not proper conduct in a given craft or profession.

2. WHAT IS ADVERTISING?

Before answering, let's consider what advertising does. In a typical ad, people are told of, or shown, various possible benefits of some service or product, usually with the aid of a gimmick or two. The gimmicks are meant to focus our consciousness and to call attention to the likely benefits of the service or product being advertised.

From this we can conclude that advertising is a form of promotion – moving something ahead positively. It is a call to people to pay attention to some service or product being offered for sale, in the hope that they may then come to want it.

Advertising is a natural extension of commerce and marketing: the promotion of what is being produced for sale.

3. ADVERTISING AS AN ARM OF BUSINESS

Institutions are extensions of human activities, organized, structured, formalized. Governments formalize self-defense and conflict adjudication; marriages formalize romance and family life; education formalizes teaching, learning and scholarship. Business is the formal expression of commerce, commerce made systematic, efficient. This is one fruitful way of understanding institutions.

Commerce, in turn, is conducted because one may well obtain benefits from it, via good deals. Commerce is, then, a form of economic prudence, making sure one gains advantages of certain (exchangeable) kinds by interaction with others who seek to do the same. Mutual advantage-seeking in matters of consumption and production is what constitutes commerce and, when formalized, doing business itself.

For commerce to take place most effectively, the parties need to promote whatever they have to offer in exchange, by calling their wares to each others' attention. Without this, they will have produced in vain and will lack resources to consume, and so they need to advertise. And business takes this a step further, by developing advertising into an adjacent institution, indeed, into a profession or specialization.

4.   MORALITY AND HUMAN INSTITUTIONS

In order to tell whether advertising can be conducted ethically, it first has to be clear that commerce and business are themselves morally appropriate. Why is it important whether commerce is morally okay? If by this you mean whether, when one embarks upon something, one is acting rightly, not wrongly, being decent or upright rather than vile or evil, then the issue is crucial in order for us to be sure we live decently and that our profession and what we utilize for making it successful do not demean us as human beings.

Suppose a person thinks about joining the US Army, the Peace Corps or Microsoft Corporation. Debates can ensue about whether these are good things and whether one does right by joining in. Pacifists criticize members of the military for having joined what they consider to be a morally flawed institution. Maybe the Peace Corps is imperialistic, invasive. Maybe corporations are materialistic and aim blindly for profit. Critics suggest this, as they suggest the moral impropriety of bull fighting, boxing or animal experimentation – they allege that these and many other human activities are morally wrong.

Socialists and communists think business is wrong. They feel that people should abstain from commerce and engage, instead, in sharing resources with one another. Profiteers are deemed little better than rapists or child molesters. The reason, according to socialists and communists – and indeed many others, though less explicitly – is that advancing oneself or one's wares via exchange is wrong – one should not embark upon self-enhancement or private enterprise by exploiting the opportunity to gain from what others need and want. One should always think of the welfare of the community or society or even humanity, and act accordingly. Anything that does not aim for this is considered morally wrong.

5. MORALITY AND COMMERCE

But if socialists, communists and others are mistaken, how would we tell? We would need to have some idea as to what makes something morally okay. And this is tough terrain to explore – philosophers and theologians have attempted it for centuries. Yet some came up with better answers than others, even if later these answers were reconsidered and modified by new generations.

If morality is a tool that enables human beings to live a good life here on earth, then the anti-commercial moral attitude is a mistake. Commerce enhances, very often, one's ability to live a good life. Accordingly, advertising does no less. It is a means by which one facilitates the effort to live prosperously, and as such it is morally okay, indeed. It is no less morally okay than going for a medical check-up or watching one's diet. No less so than driving carefully and getting exercise. It is taking care of one's well being – a form of the virtue of prudence or its subdivisions of industry and economy, as argued in the first section of this book.

6. PITFALLS OF ADVERTISING

Advertising can be excessive, as can be attention to one's health or nutrition or physique. Yet, oddly, the most extensive manifestation of advertising occurs in a medium that is not really private, not through and through, namely, television. The more natural, normal forms of advertising occur in magazines and newspapers, where there has been less of a legally protected monopoly historically than on broadcast television.

Advertising can also involve tastelessness, demeaning imagery, deceit, distortion, stereotyping, etc. But none of this is indigenous to advertising.

Sadly, in a cultural atmosphere wherein a schizophrenic attitude prevails about commerce and business, advertising is also looked at askance: rewards are given for interesting examples of it but, as an institution, it is not as respected as, say, medicine or education. Health care is praised but wealth care is demeaned.

7. THE SOURCE OF THE TROUBLE

Is there a schizophrenic attitude about commerce in much of Western culture? One need but consider how much business success is depended upon, not just for ordinary human prosperity but for those institutions where people tend largely to demean commerce, namely, higher education, the arts and so forth. And then one can reflect on the reputation of people in commerce – the dealer, the trader, the salesman, the manager, and others. All these are regarded with moral suspicion by many theologians, philosophers and other members of the literati.

Why, basically, is this the way commerce and, in consequence, advertising are regarded? The quick answer, albeit probably quite right, is also a very controversial one.

When human beings regard a part of themselves, such as the mind or spirit, as otherworldly and the rest, namely, their bodies and all that is associated with the body, mundane, and when the former is deemed noble while the latter is deemed base, business will suffer. It is no accident that Jesus became violent only against money lenders in the temple, despite the fact, noted already in this work, that there were many other sinners there, many hypocrites and others who demeaned the house of God.

There is a similarity between how business and sexuality are viewed by many. Both may be desired but they are not admired. There is a naturalistic version of this, as well. Even if all some position does is regard the mind as superior in significance to the body, this will tend to lead to regarding only activities and institutions that serve to elevate the mind as being morally worthy. The body is but a means to the worthy, lofty goal of exercising the mind. This is just how Plato and even Aristotle saw it, and thus they viewed commerce or retail trade as being morally lowly or of mere instrumental value.

Advertising is meant to advance commerce or business, and if these are deemed to facilitate the baser aspects of human life, there is no mystery as to why they are viewed with suspicion and even moral disdain.

However, living virtuously amounts to, among other matters, making sure one flourishes as a human being. And since human beings are natural – they are rational *animals* – then flourishing includes living as a successful biological entity. It requires, among other things, a balanced approach to caring for oneself and living prudently.

As a rule, then, commerce would be a way to pursue and fulfill the goal of prosperity, of wealth, something that is a serious means by which to make one's life on Earth flourish. A rational animal isn't going to be satisfied by mere survival but *by flourishing* as such an entity, which would include partaking of many of life's possibilities, including art, science, leisure, travel, entertainment and the like, all of which are unattainable without effective, well-conducted commerce and business.

If, also, commerce and business are enhanced by advertising, this shows that advertising is, as a rule, a morally respectable arm of these fields of human endeavor.

8. SOME SOURCES OF HOSTILITY TO ADVERTISING

One source of the hostility toward advertising is the notion that ads manipulate us as if we were puppets on strings. Some people believe that human beings are completely malleable – clay that can be molded by psychological techniques, gimmicks and so on. When somebody is charged with a crime, defense attorneys will often argue not that the accused didn't do it but that the accused couldn't help himself; if somebody cannot help doing what he does, he can't be guilty. Nor can he be praised, however. And if that's the case, we're all just preprogrammed robots.

Yet, underlying the whole ethical framework of human life is our awareness that people ordinarily can choose. This would be evident even in you're taking me to task for making such a claim: if you criticize me for something I do, you are assuming that I could have done otherwise.

One famous critic of advertising was the late John Kenneth Galbraith of Harvard University, who was an economist and one-time ambassador to India under the Kennedy administration. As he put it, "An even more direct link between production and wants is provided by the institutions of modern advertising and salesmanship. These cannot be reconciled with the notion of independently determined desires, for their central function is to create desires – to bring into being wants that previously did not exist."[45]

This idea has had an impact on how a number of academicians, including most business ethics scholars, think about advertising. They treat it as a weapon directed at people who are helpless to resist. But it isn't, and they aren't. Indeed, one of the reasons advertising has to be cleverly designed is that *people can ignore it*. They can walk away from commercials in a jiffy, even from the best of them. That's also why advertisers *target* their audience. They try to reach the folks who are already predisposed to buy the kind of thing they have to sell.

In the real world as we normally perceive it, we can tell very easily that advertising is not at the root of our desires. If we disdain sports, it doesn't matter how many commercials for surfboards, jerseys, and Monday night football we see. They just bounce off of us. We go buy a book instead.

F. A. Hayek argues as much when he points out that "Professor Galbraith's argument would be easily employed, without any change of the essential terms, to demonstrate the worthlessness of literature or any other form of art. Surely an individual's want for literature is not original with himself in the sense that he would experience it if literature were not produced."[46] Of course, any

---

[45]John Kenneth Galbraith, "The Dependence Effect," *The Affluent Society.*
[46]Op. cit., Hayek, "The Non Sequitur of the 'Dependence Effect.' "

response to the things of the world requires that those things first exist, prior to our response to them. There is an objective reality out there, but that is no bar to free will!

Perhaps, for Galbraith, independent determination of desire meant one must create all the products and services one might possibly want from scratch, oneself; that would, paradoxically enough, vastly curtail the range of products and services from which we could select. (Society would at least be less affluent, in that case.) But his attitude makes sense only if the whole of human action is a matter of stimulus-provoking automatic response. And if that were so, there would be no additional onus of culpability that could be imputed to advertising and to the business that produces it. Advertising would be just some amoral activity in which we engage.

Fortunately, the situation is otherwise. Far from regarding their prospects as sheep, most ad writers assume, at least implicitly, that customers will do some serious examining to find out if the product or service really does suit their purposes.

9.   THE BENEFITS OF ADVERTISING

Advertising benefits both producers and consumers. It makes possible mutually beneficial exchanges that might not have taken place otherwise.

What do advertisers accomplish for themselves when they successfully pitch a product? They will have found a way to make a living.[47] Consider the poor benighted telemarketer, calling you up in the middle of dinner with a proposal to switch your telephone service.

Do I hang up on the guy, myself? No. Partly because I'm in business ethics and think about this all the time, I take a moment to say, "No, I've got a service I'm perfectly satisfied with. Thank you, bye-bye." (As opposed to: "Get off my phone, you asshole!") Even if I'm not willing to attend to a salesman's message, I at least extend him some courtesy, because I appreciate what he is trying to do: earn a living. That is a bond between us. After all, I'm trying to earn a living, too. If I pitch my latest book at a cocktail party, I don't want to get bopped on the nose by the guy who is perfectly happy with the latest Stephen King novel and doesn't want to hear about anything else.

Others, of course, might wish never to be bothered at all with such pitches. At home, they might well have their answering machines deal with all this. There is no general, one-size-fits-all, right answer as to what we ought to do about this sort of thing, period.

---

[47] A little sympathy for junk ad mailers might be appropriate here, given what they are trying to do: make a living. They're trying to call out, "Hey! Here we are! Please, consider us as you embark on trade."

In this age of broadcasting, advertisements are often presented to many millions more than are in the market for the product or service being promoted. As one views a television or listens to a radio program, an ad interrupts, and this tends to annoy us. (Our annoyance is, incidentally, yet more evidence against the notion that advertisers can simply reconstitute our preferences at will.) Most viewers, during most commercials, would rather continue attending to the program; the ads thwart this goal.

Once in a while, of course, an ad aimed squarely at one's own needs and wants comes up, and then the benefits of advertising for human beings qua consumers begins to become clear. So perhaps one can be tolerant of ads that miss the mark. (And are there no mute buttons or TiVo?) In other contexts, when ads are more narrowly cast, they are not so annoying. Indeed, sometimes readers of specialized magazines will flip through, looking only at the ads.

Advertising also benefits us in cases where we never buy any of the products being advertised. Thanks to TV ads, we don't have to pay for network television – and the cost of cable television is less than it might be. Without ads, we would not enjoy access to so much free information on the Internet. Internet access itself is now available at no charge, as long as you're willing to put up with some pop-up ads. Advertising is thus one modern method for spreading the benefits of new products and services from the few to the many.[48]

10.   ADVERTISING AND PRUDENCE

Once both parties have done their level best to find out what will be prudent for them to do, but not before then, they may properly unite in trade.

Not everyone is always prudent, it's true. Some people just see ads and, without further ado, yield to the desire to get what is being offered; they buy on impulse. Impulse buying most closely resembles the phenomenon that Galbraith and others think advertising engenders *all* the time. But people who buy on impulse don't have to buy; they merely have chosen to do so carelessly. (And even then, the impulse buyer's imprudent purchases are confined to the realm of his already-chosen values and interests – for example, clothing, lottery tickets, food, or books.)

Just as having the capacity to reason does not mean that one will always reason, so having the capacity to be prudent does not mean that one will always practice prudence. Participants in the market can fail to be alert, fail to pay attention to their own responsibility in a trade. They may place all the responsibility in the hands of the other party to a trade and then, afterwards,

---

[48]There is, of course, no need at all for a law establishing a list of "do not call" numbers – entrepreneurs in the free market could easily cope with this matter but government has now co-opted them.

when they are eating the losses, blame that other party, not themselves. But they are complicit in so far as they neglected to pay sufficient attention to what was going down.

11.   WHAT'S A GOOD AD?

The primary responsibility of an ad is to call attention to a product in such an effective way that people will have difficulty overlooking it.

Again, why is it morally okay to try to capture people's attention this way? Because it's important for us to prosper. That means it's important for us to promote the services or wares that we have to offer for sale. If human life is a value, advertising is a value. It is a positive good.

Advertising is not selfish in any cruel, nasty, or brutal sense of the word; rather, it is *self-responsible*. People in business must make this effort to take care of themselves, to do justice to the prospect of succeeding and prospering in their lives. Everybody benefits thereby – the customers, the people who own and run the business, and the employees whom businesses are able to hire when the advertising does its work.

12.   ADVERTISING AND NUISANCE

My in-flight magazine had a piece on telemarketing, condemning it all as some kind of major intrusion in one's life, with the article framed by advertise-ments on each side of it. I was reading the lambaste and thinking about how inconsistent the author and editor could be, finding such grievous fault with those who try to drum up business via the phone but none at all for doing it on the pages of the magazine where the lambaste is being advanced. It reminds me of all the corporate bashing done in Hollywood movies (such as 'Wall Street' and 'Erin Brockovich') that are produced by, you guessed it, major corpora-tions. As Lenin said, the capitalists will sell you the ropes with which you plan to hang them. Well, at least some of them will. No one should ever believe that all people in business know what is needed to keep the integrity of the business system intact.

Okay – we have already noted that telephone advertisers are a bit of a pain, especially if they call at bad times, which can be different, of course, for dif-ferent people. But, as I have already noted, they are just asking for a little time to try to make a living.

But there is a kind of aggressive advertising that does deserve condemna-tion, good and hard. It is when you are trying to reach some outfit – for infor-mation and correcting a mistake they have made with your bill, or some such problem – you are put on 'hold' and have to endure a steady flow of screaming in your ear while you are holding, so as to reach the department with which you need to do business they want from you!

Why is this different from all other kinds of advertising? Because, while you are waiting on hold, you normally cannot go anywhere to escape the barrage of messages you have decided right away that you do not want to hear. Sometimes, if you have a speaker-phone option on your telephone, you can just have those messages play to the air, while you keep half an ear open and get back when someone finally answers, but even that is close to being entrapped, since you must endure it to some measure. But the worst of it is when you have nowhere to go and have to wait in order to get the business accomplished, and they keep pumping the stuff into your ear mercilessly.

Since I haven't a clue as to how this can be circumvented, my only way to deal with it is to accost whoever eventually comes on line, and tell them what I think of this entrapment. Not that it will do much good. But this is the way I am my own Ralph Nader, for better or worse. (I am thinking of inventing a gadget that will put them on hold for a while when they come on the line, blasting messages at them about what I might be able to do for them, for a nice charge.)

But this is not to denounce all advertising as nasty or vile; quite the contrary. It is intended to point up that some of it is quite benign, indeed, and amounts to no more than other people's peaceful efforts to reach out and solicit livelihood, while some of it is genuinely intrusive. Anyone who gets bent out of shape about all ads would seem to me to be rather mean-minded. Even junk mail should not be denounced – you can toss it easily enough and if you understand that it amounts to nothing more or less than people's efforts to make a living, how can you be mad at it? But then, of course, this is part of the problem with the anti-business, anti-commercial mentality: it tends to denounce efforts to live well, even to live! For what is business but the institutional, professional expression of a large portion of that desire?

On the other hand, when someone traps you into having to listen to a pitch, even though you have no interest in it at all, that's something else entirely. And that is what those blasted messages are, when you are on 'hold,' waiting to get a reservation booked with an airline or a billing question answered from a credit card company. Even having their choice of music funneled into my ear is something I protest!

13. POLETOWN BLUES

As a teacher of business ethics, I receive a good deal of literature of the business-bashing variety that passes for study material. For example, I used to be bombarded with advertising for a "documentary" film entitled *Poletown Lives*, a "Blue Ribbon Winner" at the American Film Festival in New York in 1983, a film that was later famous as class material in so-called business ethics courses.

There are several issues that the promotion of this film for class use raises for me. For one, those promoting the material seem to assume that people who teach courses in business – including ethics, anthropology, communications, economics, history, political science, social work, sociology, urban studies and similar subjects – really want to show materials that amount to little more than propaganda. I would think most professors prefer to show materials that cover several sides of a controversy, rather than just one side. It is also assumed by the promoters that a project which merits a film prize is automatically good educational material. Most importantly, however, something else is wrong with this movie.

The case of Poletown gains its relevance mostly from the fact, pointed out in Joseph Auerbach's 1985 *Harvard Business Review* essay, "The Poletown Dilemma," that General Motors Corporation was able to make use of the *eminent domain* law to gain land in Poletown to build an assembly plant. Yet, none of the promotional literature calls attention to this fact. Mostly what is stressed, not only in the promotional literature but also in the film, is that General Motors has immense power to influence politics.

Emphasizing this fact about the case, however, is to focus on something that's not actually all that important. What is more important, by far, is the legal infrastructure that made Poletown's problems nearly inevitable.

Let us recall that the eminent domain law – the "takings clause" of the Fifth Amendment to the U.S. Constitution – concerns "taking private property for public purposes." Yet this law is entirely misapplied when the purpose for which private property is taken is in fact something private, such as General Motors' economic success. There is nothing in the 5th Amendment of the U.S. Constitution that authorizes such use of the "takings" clause. The eminent domain tradition, interpreted honestly, concerns the need of governments to do their unique business – build court houses, police stations, and military facilities. None of that implies that government has any authority to use eminent domain to do favors for special groups, especially at the expense of other special groups, nor that this legal instrument may be used to violate private property rights in order to increase tax revenues.[49]

But, of course, those who complain about the Poletown incident will not likely blame government. They are not apt to object in principle to eminent domain usage of this kind. After all, government's taking private property for such private uses as to build museums, swimming pools, parks, and so forth is often just fine with most critics of corporate power. What they don't like is when government uses the eminent domain provision *in favor of business!*

---

[49]For an excellent discussion, see op. cit., Greenhut, *Abuse of Power.*

Business is not to be honored with the legal privilege to reap such special favors, even while other aspects of culture are. But it is naïve to believe that the abuse of eminent domain can be resisted when it favors business but not when it favors other endeavors. The law does not work that way.

I will gladly show the Poletown propaganda film in my classes in business ethics when it presents a principled and fair-minded discussion of the issues involved. But if all I get is badmouthing of General Motors – that is, American business – I will regard the film as nothing more than a bigoted outlash against a perfectly legitimate aspect of human culture, namely commerce. That businesses take just as vigorous advantage of government's willingness to subvert its proper role of protecting the rights of citizens and engage in serving special-interest goals is no news at all – everybody these days is doing that kind of thing! And, sadly, the US Supreme Court has given this legitimacy via its 5 to 4 ruling in the Kelo *v.* New London, CT (Summer, 2005).

14.   JOURNALISM V. BUSINESS

Here are two perfectly normal, familiar professions – journalism and business. Yet the former is treated with kid gloves by many intellectuals, politicians and academics, while the latter is routinely condemned *en masse*.

Consider that when the Enron corporate scandal broke, the mantra of most commentators was how it was all due to the fact of deregulation. If only the federal government took it upon itself to rein in all those allegedly greedy corporate executives, if only it never yielded to the call for lessening the meddling it used to perpetrate, if only we returned to the feudal practice of mercantilism – whereby the king's court routinely micro-managed the country's business – we would be a much more just, decent society.

But now consider CBS-TV's *60 Minutes* fiasco, involving former anchorman Dan Rather. Not only do these folks get away with stonewalling about what happened, not only does Rather issue but a lame "I am sorry" – which, by the way, isn't necessarily an apology but could well be a mere "it's too bad it happened" – but no one is calling, as indeed no one ought to, for re-instituting the age-old (and often still accepted) practice of government regulation – censorship – of the press.

This is very interesting. To begin with, there is an inconsistency in our federal constitution. It authorizes the feds to regulate nearly every profession except for journalism and the ministry. The First Amendment, while a great principle, is plainly discriminatory. If two professions of vital importance to a society are protected from government intrusion, it is rank injustice to subject other professions to such intrusiveness.

But in the case of Dan Rather & Co., it gets more complicated – television operates on "public" property and is, therefore, not fully protected from the feds, after all. This is why the Federal Communications Commission (FCC) is empowered to impose various rules on radio and television broadcasters, say, about advertising, "appropriate" language, running of public service announcements, children's programming, and so forth. The news divisions are excluded from FCC interference mainly as a matter of tradition, not law. Strictly speaking, the FCC could make rules for them, also, since they, too, are using "public" property – the electromagnetic spectrum which was nationalized by the US Senate back in 1927.

Yet, despite this power of the feds over broadcasters, no sane person is demanding that the FCC issue government regulations concerning broadcast news. We all know that this would violate a most cherished aspect of what is left of our free society. Censorship of the press is simply too Draconian a form of tyranny for the government to risk – it might show just where exactly governments are so often inclined to go!

Still, just because it would look bad to call for it, it doesn't follow, logically speaking, that it isn't exactly what many commentators should be calling for, given how readily they call for government regulation of people in business, industry, and other professions when something goes amiss there. Alas, consistency is deemed to be the hobgoblin of little minds. (Actually, however, it is "a foolish consistency" that Emerson was talking about, not consistency, plain and simple, which really amounts to integrity, nothing less.)

Journalists, sadly, are deemed to be some kind of select elite, not deserving of the disdain in which people in business are held – or perhaps it is the other way around: people in business are held in low esteem, as a class, while journalists and ministers – can you really grasp this in our day, what with hundreds of members of the clergy being exposed as out-and-out scum? – are treated simply as normal folk, some of whom will be bad apples now and then. In fact, however, members of all professions, educators, scientists, artists, business folks, journalists, you name them, are pretty much the same. They are all capable of going bad, and of being corrupted.

In a genuinely free society, this is a risk we ought all to accept, and we should not assume that government is populated by saints who should be entrusted to be the armed guardians of us all. In such a society, all aspects of culture, including commerce, are free of the coercive guidance of government, and receive what all citizens are entitled to, once they form a legal order, namely, the protection of their rights.

Wealthcare, just as health and any other form of caring for some aspect of human life, needs to be carried out by the free citizenry, not by a Nanny State.

Chapter 6

JOBS IN A FREE COUNTRY

1.   THE MYTH OF JOB SECURITY

From naïve cinematic sentiment to official public ideology is unfortunately not that big a leap. Once during the New Hampshire primaries, former President Bill Clinton was stumping with a speech, part of which was aired on National Public Radio. The president took many of his lines from the funny Kevin Kline movie "Dave." In it, the fictional presidential stand-in, played by Kline, proclaims his intention of securing a job for everyone in the country.

A few years later, President George W. Bush was making a similar pledge in his acceptance speech at the 2004 Republican National Convention. "To create more jobs in America, America must be the best place in the world to do business. To create jobs, my plan will encourage investment and expansion by restraining federal spending, reducing regulation and making the tax relief permanent. To create jobs, we will make our country less dependent on foreign sources of energy. To create jobs, we will expand trade and level the playing field to sell American goods and services across the globe."

There is, in fact, no way for Clinton, Bush or any other politician to literally "create jobs," not, at least, without also destroying them. All a government can do is reduce obstacles to economic growth, to investment and entrepreneurship. Arguably, government is in fact the main obstacle to the creation of jobs, by way of its taxation and regulation, and protectionism.[50] When taxes are levied, people have less to spend, and this means companies need fewer workers to create the smaller amount of goods and services that customers can now afford to purchase. When regulations are imposed, enormous amounts of money are spent by government on carrying out this regulatory function – with huge staffs, massive overhead, and the unrelenting intrusiveness that treats economic agents as if they were guilty without any proof of

---

[50]Taxation takes resources from citizens who would most likely have wanted to spend it one something other than what the government will spend it for. (For more, see Tibor R. Machan, *Libertarianism Defended* [Burlington, VT: Ashgate, 2006].) Regulation imposes burdens on people who haven't violated anyone's rights. (See, for a detailed discussion, Tibor R. Machan, "The Petty Tyrannies of Government Regulation," in M. B. Johnson & T. R. Machan, eds., *Rights and Regulation* [Boston, MA: Ballinger Books, 1983].) Protectionism bars people from purchasing goods and services at lower prices, thus preventing them from spending for other goods and services.

having done anyone any harm at all. And firms must employ teams of attorneys and human resources staff with which to cope with such regulations, either complying with them or dodging them as best they can. All this is a dead weight on the economy.

Some believe that protectionism saves jobs but what it actually does is stifle competition from businesses abroad, thus allowing domestic firms to charge more than what products or services would fetch in a free market and thus taking money from customers that they could spend on, among other things, creating jobs for people. There are some transition problems in a free economy, of course, but these are minor compared to the massive waste engendered by protectionism.

It is only be removing such obstacles that one can create better job prospects – not jobs themselves but the prospect of them. There is no guarantee that even if they have greater funds and suffer fewer obstacles, persons will actually spend and invest. Certain economic theories hold that people are hard-wired to seek out good deals; that they are in perpetual economizing motion. But persons clearly are not thus hard-wired. Human beings are distinctive in the living world precisely for their capacity to *choose* what they will do.[51]

Still, the likelihood that people will stimulate economic growth is far greater without all the governmental obstructionism than with it. And on that score President George W. Bush was quite correct. It does bear emphasis, though, that politicians cannot create jobs – and that when they make the more brazen promise that they will do just that, they reveal themselves to be either terribly confused or duplicitous.

Jobs are created when people choose to purchase goods and services and other people choose to create and sell those goods and services to meet that demand. Period. When government "creates" jobs, it must either attempt to force people to buy things they do not want, or else outright rob them of their resources and use these resources to engage in artificial purchases, public works, expenditures, and investments. By the very nature of such policies, they create unwanted jobs and displace the wanted ones, imposing a drag on the economy. Men and women may comply with laws coercing them to purchase products and services at the expense of the products and services they would prefer or at higher prices than they would otherwise have to pay; but they naturally resist the compulsion and seek ways to circumvent it.[52]

Job creation, in short, is not a political task. It is our own everyday task, what we do when we go shopping. Moreover, no one can give another person

---

[51] For more, see Tibor R. Machan, *Putting Humans First, Why We Are Nature's Favorite* (Lanham, MD: Rowman & Littlefield, 2004).

[52] Businesses and individuals invest inordinate sums in legal services that make it possible for them to do this.

job security, not unless someone else is placed into involuntary servitude – which is the "security" of chains.[53] To secure a demand for some productive activity in the marketplace, others must make the free choice to purchase, repeatedly, the result. This means that by the very nature of the process, there is no way whatever to guarantee a job for anyone if potential customers are treated as sovereign, free agents; those who are free to buy are also free not to buy.[54] If, however, job security is promised to us, those who make such a promise cannot treat customers as sovereign, free agents but as slaves to the products that must be purchased to secure the jobs in question.

I have been, among other things, a tenured university professor at large state universities. Only by committing a crime could I have been fired or laid off, unless the entire institution were abolished by the politicians of my state. I could enjoy job security only by forcing the taxpayers to give up their income for the sake of my own goal, that of teaching college level philosophy courses. My job was secure only because others were and continue to be placed into involuntary servitude for the sake of supplying the productive service of college teaching. I lived off their involuntary service, extracted from them in the form of taxes – that is, the forcible relinquishing of a portion of their earnings – each April 15th.

Can this be just and right? Many think education is so important that people ought to be forced to pay to produce it, never mind their own choices in the matter. This is just one of those times when talk about what "we" want hides the fact that some people may well *not* want it, so that the "we" really is just "some of us," with others being enlisted by dint of coercion. In a relatively free society bits and pieces of such enforced job security may survive. But even these instances are somewhat illusory since, after all, the majority of voters may at some point change their minds and pull the employment rug out from under the tenured professors. Indeed, this has already happened at some colleges and universities, which have abandoned promising tenure and even reneged on past commitments inasmuch as the money just wasn't there to stoke this job security myth. Be that as it may, to promise job security to all workers – as Clinton and the fictional Dave did and even Bush was verging on doing – is outright deception.

In a society in which the rights to freedom of labor movement and consumer choice are respected and protected, no one can deliver "job security." A com-

---

[53]The exception would be the rare individual or firm of inordinate wealth able to offer a contract that amounts to tenure.

[54]John Kenneth Galbraith argues that advertising makes us captives of sellers, depriving us of our sovereignty by creating within us a desire – actually, a compulsion – to buy the advertised products and services. See, John Kenneth Galbraith, *The Affluent Society* (1965). Cf., F. H. Hayek, "The Non-Sequitor of 'The Dependence Effect'," in Tom L. Beachamp & Norman E. Bowie, eds., *Ethical Theory and Business* (Englwood Cliffs, NJ: Prentice Hall, 1983).

pany would be lying if it made such a commitment. How would they keep their customers coming back for their product regardless of any future preferences of those customers – at the point of a gun? Yet that is exactly what would be needed to deliver on such a promise. And even then, the enforcers themselves might go on strike! If the trend toward compulsion is widespread, eventually a country's economy can collapse from lack of personal initiative. The promise is phony in any society. But it is especially phony in a society that pretends to afford some measure of citizen – including consumer – sovereignty.[55]

Wishful thinking has won many an election though; and, no doubt, without some alternative and realistic vision to take its place, the fraudulent ideal of job security will continue to gain sizable support in American electoral politics. But that ideal is corrupt. Which means we will pay the price of pursuing it – or rather, our children will, when attempts to institute forced labor in society result in the stagnation that must in time arrive.

2.   JOB VOLATILITY

Karl Marx argued that as a matter of historical necessity, capitalism would eventually collapse and give rise to socialism. Many now believe he was wrong, but they rest their disagreement not so much on any problem discerned in his theory as on the failure of the Soviet attempt to faithfully enough implement it. Actually, Marx himself would probably have denied that the Soviets could make an effective go of socialism. He warned that if socialism were attempted in places where capitalism had never had a chance to develop, this would only accomplish the "socialization of poverty" – exactly what happened in the Soviet bloc.[56]

Whether Marx had anything of enduring importance to say about the future of capitalism cannot be settled here.[57] But there is one point he clearly had right. He noted that in capitalism many workers could get fed up with the system because of its volatility, especially when it comes to job security. In a capitalist economy, there is what Marx called economic anarchy, by which he meant that what is bought and sold, where, and for how much, are unplanned and unpredictable. It all depends on supply and demand, and that includes the supply of and demand for labor. Workers suffer the down side of this anarchy when their jobs dry up simply because former customers decide to buy stuff

---

[55]It is widely acknowledged that the Soviet Union collapsed because its rulers made but failed to deliver on such a promise.

[56]Karl Marx had argued that for socialism to succeed, a society must first experience capitalism. Without this, what would be socialized is not wealth but poverty.

[57]For more, see Tibor R. Machan, *Revisiting Marxism, A Bourgeois Critique* (Lanham, MD: Hamilton Books, 2005).

other than what the now-unemployed workers are producing, or at least buy it in a different location in different amounts and so forth. So, in a pure capitalist market, working people may have to pull up roots and move elsewhere to prosper, or learn to make something new. Capitalism is, in this sense, destructive of stability.

Of course, workers themselves also benefit enormously from this "anarchy," not only as customers but as workers: employment is far more abundant under capitalism than it is under any known alternative. This is evident today if we compare employment figures from much of social democratic Europe with those from across the semi-capitalist United States. While jobs may be more stable in Europe (at least over a certain time period and for some people) than they are in America, it's a lot easier to get a job in America, because of its anarchic capitalism. If one believes, however, that all human beings require stability, must be well-rooted – so that they can live in the same place for an extended period of time, send their kids to the same schools they attended, go to the same church, and so on – then one will think badly of capitalism and wish to sacrifice its principles of free trade and limited government.

Marx believed that workers would begin to overturn capitalism as they suffered from being uprooted. They would overturn it by voting for politicians who would enact measures to "stabilize" the economy via government intervention and restriction on the use of private property. And Marx probably had it right about some people; many seem intent upon restricting trade, interfering with the movement of capital and labor, rather than risking having to adjust to volatile market pressures – which is to say, to the fact that other people do not conduct themselves in ways that always suit one's own economic goals. It's for these reasons that protectionist policies are prevalent.[58]

But what if people are far more adaptable than Marx believed? What if many of us are quite able to adjust to new social and economic conditions, even as others would make stasis legally mandatory? In the modern world there is ample evidence that people can be quite happy while on the move. Mobility is nearly the norm, at least for a great many of us, while being rooted in various communities is more of a preference than a necessity. If this fact is indicative of how people are – that they have no innate need to remain in one place, however much they may sometimes prefer this – then any attempt to restrain trade and tame the anarchy of capitalism is unjustified on such grounds. Sure, this doesn't mean people will not enjoin politicians to protect their vested interests, thereby shortsightedly sacrificing the principle of liberty for the sake of mere immediate convenience.[59]

---

[58] Social life is, of course, replete with this problem – many a lover has had his or her hopes crushed because the beloved refuses to reciprocate. Of course, often there is harmony of interests, as well, when free men and women interact.

[59] This manifests one of the problems associated with a one-size-fits-all mentality.

People often violate principles of right conduct so as to have their way. But it is wrong to do so and a failure of nerve, to boot.

3.   COMPARING MERITS OF ECONOMIC SYSTEMS

In the many years of defending the consistently free-market economy its champions have been hampered by the simple fact that no such thing exists. Like ideal marriages, genuine free markets are mostly something we can conceive of and understand in theory but rarely encounter in unadulterated form in the actual world. Yet, just as with ideal marriages, we can surely ask whether free markets, if they did exist, would be better for us all than some other conception of economic life, like mercantilism, socialism, the welfare state or communism. And we can also think through how nearly-free-market systems operate by reference to the pure free market ideal and various thought experiments, as well as the history of more-or-less-free-market societies to date.

In a free market, consumers "drive" the economy to a considerable extent. Of course, consumers are also producers. But on its face, when producers enter a market, they will go under unless consumers purchase their wares. Critics of the free market idea maintain, however, that the system is rigged in favor of big corporations, which are greedy players. Corporate managers control sizable resources because their clients, shareholders (investors, stockholders, or family members who own closed firms), have entrusted these to them. Such critics are especially outraged by the sizable salaries paid to some CEOs and a few other company managers. Many hold that something must be wrong if such people can garner huge incomes, sometimes even when the company isn't doing very well, while ordinary employers earn but a fraction of what these folks rake in. This surely cannot be the result of mere consumer choices, or so the critics reason. They are convinced that there must be something corrupt or grossly unfair afoot. So they tend to approve of various government – coercive – efforts to make the system more fair and just.

It cannot be reasonably denied that there can be malpractice in any profession, including business and, indeed, big business. We have witnessed much malfeasance throughout history. Yet, misdeeds abound in all professions – medicine has its quacks or charlatans, education its indoctrinators and deadbeat scholars, politics its demagogues and petty tyrants. Virtue and vice tend to be pretty evenly distributed among the various careers upon which folks can embark. Yet, most disparities in pay are driven by the free choices of consumers, up and down the line of the business community. This is akin to many other fields of work.

Consider that orchestra conductors get much higher pay than, say, the violinists or viola players; or that champion sluggers in baseball get much higher pay than those with mediocre records in the field, let alone ball boys and others employed by the team owners. There are only so many people in the professional sports, music, movie or book industries who are in wide demand, with the rest lagging far behind. The star system is nearly ubiquitous, and that is mostly because of how consumers of the various products and services choose to spend their resources.

Academics are hardly exempt from the consequences of such choices. A good scholar may have authored dozens of books and edited several more, yet none may have hit the big time. A modest newspaper columnist gets a pittance compared to what major columnists such as George Will or Michael Kinsley earn. Much as we all may well enjoy the fame and the huge income, those not read widely and thus paid serious money can only shrug their shoulders at this. There need be nothing more insidious going on than that millions of people want to read those few prominent writers, while far fewer are interested in what those neglected ones produce.

Is any of this necessarily unfair? No it is not, not at all. That's because none of these non-buyers of the columns of the less popular writers *owe* those writers anything. If you aren't owed the same consideration being paid to others, there is nothing unfair about the lower consideration you receive. (One does owe positive benefits to others if one has made a clear commitment to them. As a teacher, for example, one does owe each of one's student equal attention, since one has made that promise when one signed up to teach them. One does not owe this, however, to those to whom no such promises was made.)

The free market, like life itself, isn't about getting a predetermined "fair" outcome to be established without reference to the actual legitimate choices people make as they go about their own daily lives and pursue their own purposes. Yet at the end of the day the free market comes closer to giving us all a fair shake than any alternative. No socialist or near-socialist system has ever managed to distribute power and wealth without some folks at the top getting to be much better off than most others. On that score, at least, the free market is quite "fair" – we all have a pretty good chance of "getting into the game," provided we keep at it and don't proceed as if the world owes us a living. But too many of think the world does owe us a living, that whoever has a lot more than the rest has a moral and should have a legal duty to share the "surplus."[60]

4.   MORE ABOUT 'LOSING' A JOB

As Tom Brokaw, NBC-TV's now retired "Nightly News" anchor, was reporting on the loss of jobs in several western Illinois towns, I received a call from a telemarketing firm trying to sell me a new credit card. I picked up the

---

[60] See, for more on this, James P. Sterba, *Triumph Of Practice Over Theory In Ethics* (New York: Oxford University Press, 2004), his most recent discussion of the topic.

phone, listened to the pitch and said, "Sorry, I am trying to cut down on my use of credit cards," and hung up. By my refusal to purchase the new card I was no doubt contributing to some downsizing at a financial institution. By my refusal to make extensive use of credit cards and my general cut back on purchases, I was no doubt contributing to job losses somewhere in the world, perhaps even in western Illinois. If the world "owes [somebody] a living," I am one of the residents of the world defaulting on that obligation.

But when the "Nightly News" reporter visited the towns where the people were losing their jobs, we heard several interviewees denounce not the buying – or, rather, the non-buying – public like yours truly, but rather the companies that cut back on jobs to remain profitable at some level, deliver some return to investors. Neither Brokaw nor the crew of "60 Minutes" came after me with questions about why I was adopting habits so injurious to the jobs of my fellow man.

It is not CEOs who lay off employees, ultimately, but customers. We are the ones who turn to another vendor for the goods and services we want, abandoning those from whom we used to buy; or who decide to cut down on our purchases, save the money, and redistribute it, directly or by way of bank deposits, to enterprises that are in demand by customers somewhere. Being laid off is a message from customers, one that happens to be delivered by the personnel department in the company the wares of which are no longer wanted by those customers. But this elementary fact is somehow not grasped by millions of people whose jobs evaporate after customers make new decisions, change their buying habits. So they wish to retaliate when their wishes are thwarted, and do so against the messenger.

Perhaps many people are simply loathe to blame those who behave exactly as they do. Most of us when we go shopping have no compunction about switching alliances. We are quite ruthless about it. Sure, for a while we shop at Wal-Mart, but then we switch to Sears, then to J. C. Penney. We flip from Good Guys to Radio Shack. Or we stop attending baseball games and begin frequenting tennis matches. The switching game goes on and on and on, uninterrupted, and nearly everyone plays it. Who really buys the same basket of supplies and recreation, in the same amounts, from the same vendors, unvaryingly, week after week, month after month, year after year, decade after decade? How many people really insist on still always lighting their way by lantern and candle, once electricity and the light bulb have become generally available?

Employees who lose their jobs also engage in the switching game. They wouldn't want it any other way. When they decide that money they have been regularly spending on X should now be spent on Y, they wouldn't tolerate anyone ordering them to do otherwise. Consumer freedom is taken for granted, and no one would think of messing with it. Yet it is, largely, just this freedom that renders the free market so volatile. Sure, there are more insidious causes too – governments often step in and wield quite a lot of economic power when they close down some road, decide to declare some shop a blight on the community, or otherwise intervene in ways that are usually sudden and not easy to prepare for. But most such volatility originates in consumers who do nothing more sinister than alter their buying habits.

Perhaps if educators spent a bit more time teaching young people about these elementary economic facts, more people would echo the outlook of one citizen who told NBC that it would be best to stop lamenting the departure of old-line firms from the neighborhood and build new industries. "Perhaps we should stop counting on 1600 jobs from one company and instead develop 100 times 16 jobs from numerous small, local businesses." But, for some, that may sound a little too much like accepting the facts of life for comfort.

5.   GOVERNMENT AND JOBS

The impact of customers on market trends is extensive. Even when companies leave the country to produce their goods and services, in a free-market world this would happen mainly because customers have made clear that they will not purchase the products at the higher prices required by higher domestic costs of production. If domestic merchants could make the same profits from expending the same production costs domestically that they make from overseas production, they would have no motive to produce overseas.

Of course, we do not live in a free-market world by a long shot. Sure, sometimes innovation and entrepreneurship drive established companies out of business. When CDs hit the market, customers abandoned cassette tapes in droves, so that those who made those tapes had to find new work. But that's only part of the story. In the world as it is, with a vast number of laws and regulations hampering the free flow of commerce – including, of course, the flow of labor – there are many other, more artificial causes for the loss of jobs, of the sort having to do with why Arnold Schwarzenegger got elected governor of California: the inhospitable business climate in so many regions of America.

Everywhere businesses must jump through endless hoops to begin or continue production: one license after another, one permit after another, accompanied by zillions of forms to be filled out daily, as well as fees to be paid to fund, for example, workers' compensation programs. Of course, all this is legal, in the sense that courts have authorized the hoops, but this isn't the issue here. What is important for our purposes is whether these hoops ought to be legal and if we judge by the ideas of the US Declaration of Independence, and by the underlying philosophy of individual rights, these hoops are wrongheaded and discriminatory. (For example, journalists and the clergy are no subjected to such regulations.)

Then there are all the pressure groups – with their teams of lawyers – that must be appeased. Under the weight of such burdens, several high-profile businesses have left the states in which these hoops have been increasing for others, such as Nevada and Louisiana that have less Draconian regulatory measures, making clear that it was the plethora of government regulations that induced them to move.

Sadly, economic ignorance and the sheer unwillingness to think these matters through, has led a great many employees and their champions to despise company executives when these employees either lose their jobs or must move away from the neighborhoods in which they like to live. Instead of seeing the government's near-Draconian regulations as the culprit, they blame the "greed" of the managers and investors. But they are sadly mistaken. By insisting that government impose measures that benefit them even as companies are thereby squeezed beyond repair, these folks urge the transformation of a relatively free American market economy into the quasi-socialist European model in which unemployment is in the double digits and entrepreneurial activity is practically nil. When government forces companies to provide employees with life-time benefits, who can afford to start up a business?

One consequence is the gradual elimination around the country of small businesses whose owners just cannot afford to comply with all the regulations or staff huge legal departments so that these regulations might be cleverly circumvented. Indeed, it is pro-regulation champions, led by the likes of Ralph Nader, who help promote the growth of huge corporations. Only such large firms can stand up to the government and the trial lawyers who use regulations to subdue business.

So, while in a free-market economy it is ultimately the customer who is king, in the halfway house of the government-regulated mixed economy, the people who cause most job losses are the promoters and executors of government regulations. If politicians really want to do something about rescuing the country from economic demise, let them not only cut taxes – of course a good thing to do in any case – but also repeal the laws that burden and often outright bury so many businesses.

6.   JOBS AND TECHNOLOGY

Where I live the trash is now picked up almost completely mechanically. The truck drives up and stops, and the driver pushes a button that causes mechanical arms to reach out, scoop the huge trash container, lift it in the air and dump the contents into the truck's compactor.

A crime? Once upon a time, three or four people ran around collecting the trash, lifting the container manually to dump the contents into the truck. If we are to believe John Kerry, John Edwards and it seems the entire Democratic

Party of the United States of America, as well as their academic apologists, whoever invented that mechanical contraption must be a lowly criminal. After all, he robbed all the folks who used to pick up the trash of their jobs! Just absconded with them.

Never mind that at the same time new jobs opened up at the plants where these mechanical contraptions are being manufactured. Never mind that there are now people making the new, technologically more sophisticated trucks, administering the requisite paperwork entailed, guarding the plants and so forth – doing all the jobs that didn't exist before. These folks, too, must be in cahoots with the thieves, of course, since they are beneficiaries of the loss of jobs suffered by the trash crews that are no longer needed in our neighborhood.

That such implications are patent nonsense doesn't prevent them from being peddled almost this explicitly by politicians counting on monumental economic ignorance to get elected and enact laws and regulations only a Luddite could love. Luddites were 19th-century British workers who went about destroying money-saving machines that replaced manual laborers. They thought that the introduction of these machines must be a plot against working people who were indeed being laid off and replaced by the nefariously capable machines.

It didn't occur to the Luddites that the time and money thus saved could then be spent on new devices and contraptions, creating new goods and services, all of which require the creation of new jobs if they are to be produced and marketed. We have even less excuse for accepting their delusions today. For if the introduction of any new labor-saving machinery indeed permanently trimmed the sum total of jobs, an industrial and technological economy like that of the United States would be suffering 95% instead of 5% unemployment.

Few of the jobs available in 2005 resemble those available in 1805; so, clearly, the innovations that render an economy more productive do not ipso facto shrink that more-productive economy. Thinking it through logically would, of course, have informed the Luddites about how these things work out. They would have realized that losing your job as hunter-gatherer doesn't mean that civilization and job markets must now grind to a halt. But thinking it through was too much trouble. It was easier to see only what stared them in the face, namely, that some people were no longer doing a particular job that they used to do. The costs of the Luddites' particular labor-saving device – i.e., the device and expedient of omitting time-consuming logic and evidence from one's deliberations – far outweigh any imagined benefits.

It's possible that many of the displaced workers apprehend such lines of thought at least vaguely, but simply cannot come to grips with having to improve their skills to meet the needs of a changing marketplace. This is what is most frightening – that all those who pitch their misguided economic views may be intentionally catering to the laziest and most recalcitrant folks in the labor force, those flatly unwilling to cope with the reasonable requirements of making a living in a vibrant and evolving free economy.

Now, of course, many of us get into mindless routines and begin to wish that the world would just calm down so we need no longer bother with learning new skills or revising old habits. Maybe in our later years this is thought to be prudent – after all, the exigencies of keeping up with the "rat race" can seem rather exasperating.

But what about the virtue of old dogs learning some new tricks? What about living in the present and not the obsolete past? Even apart from the narrow-minded ideology contra "loss of jobs" begrudges the world the benefits of innovation, what about the benefits of forestalling one's own premature mental and physical retirement? Is it really such a wonderful thing to sink lethargically into a state of stasis – in other words, to rot?

I doubt it. And our politicians should not be so eager to cater to those who prefer to stand still and prevent the rest of us from moving forward, from improving ways of living and working.

7.   BETTER AND WORSE JOBS, AND LETTERS

If one wishes to come up with examples of support for misguided policies by government, keeping one's eye on the pages of many major newspapers will help. One such supportive opinion appeared in *The New York Times Magazine*, March 7, 2004, where a letter writer proceeds as follows:

> "But not all jobs are created equal. Working in a unionized factory with good pay, affordable health care and a pension is not the same as giving facials for $7 an hour without benefits or job security. Sure, manicurists and others should be counted in national job figures. But we should also be clear that the jobs created in these areas generally don't pay enough or provide the kind of benefits needed to raise a family. The debate about manufacturing jobs lost isn't just about numbers; it's about quality too."

What then follows from this? Only that it would be better for them if people had higher than lower quality jobs. Anyone over 5 years of age knows this. Unless, of course, the writer, who was taking issue with an explanation of what happens when jobs are outsourced to other countries, intended by his words to give support to protectionism or to unraveling free-trade policies – I mean the genuine ones that make it possible for people across the globe to compete with one another for the patronage of various consumers. But that conclusion, of course, doesn't follow from the letter writer's laments.

America is no longer isolated from competition, just as no region in America has for long been isolated from other regions. Previously, outsourcing went from one state to another, one city to the other and so forth, usually based, in part, on where one could find more competitive labor and location prices. This is still going on, just in case someone is eager to make a case for domestic protectionism.

Protectionism, as already noted, coerces costumers to buy at a higher price than they could without it. Thus governments create a bit of job security for some people – those who are unwilling to work for less or to move somewhere else or learn a new set of job skills – by barring trade. Protectionism thus attempts to make *involuntary servants* of customers by forcing them to work for those who want to keep their jobs regardless of what customers want.

It is hard to imagine a more wrongheaded, immoral economic notion afoot today. People worry about child labor, as if that in itself violates basic human rights – which it doesn't unless forced upon families and children by the state. Yet it is far more insidious to secure people's jobs not because they have something better or cheaper to offer but because they have managed to enlist the military and police powers of government to bar competitors (for example, in farm products).

In the past a few countries had been something of a job heaven because others were greater or lesser tyrannies that didn't permit business to flourish in their midst. Now this is coming to an end, and the entire world community is entering the same marketplace more or less rapidly. This greater freedom throughout various markets means there will be new competitors, ones who can bid lower than others in the previously privileged countries. Once the job market is widened, there will be newcomers who will outbid the existing group of workers. That is what competition means, and any effort to keep the newcomers out is comparable to how the Mafia does "business," not how free men and women are supposed to.[61]

Of course, there are various factors aside from expansion of the labor market that figure in all this, some of them pretty nasty – such as the already mentioned extortionist taxation and regulation that makes it impossible for businesses to keep wages high while also remaining competitive. But that is clearly not the concern of the letter writer above, nor of others who root for protectionism.

Now and then, of course, one finds support for the idea of free competition in America even apart from economists who tend to know well enough the damage such a public policy inflicts on people. One recent e-mail gives one some hope:

> "Your explanation as to the 'why' of losing certain types of jobs is one of the best … [T]he example [of] … trash handlers is not only down to earth but also that if anyone doesn't have an better understanding of the issue after reading your piece, he or she just doesn't want to understand the dynamics involved."

---

[61]This process may be compared to how the American basketball ("dream") team used to win with great ease until some others, such as the Yugoslavs and Russians, caught up to them and they no longer dominated the sport.

8.   OUTSOURCING: THE OBJECTIONS

I have recently penned more than a few essays and columns about job security and "outsourcing," and these have prompted more than a few readers
to respond. Some are very supportive of my free-market analysis, but a rather
large group weighs in with everything from thoughtful objections to vitriolic
diatribes. Now, my default policy is to read all such posts, but if the first line
contains an insult – name-calling, nasty attribution of motives, or the always
heartening "go back to your native country" kind of shameful outburst – I do
not read the rest and just send back a post saying so.

What is worthy of a response is the observation that much of the job outsourcing we see is due to wrongheaded domestic and foreign governmental
policy. Those critics stress the point that outsourcing – in this context "hiring
the services of people abroad rather than continuing to employ those in the
home country" – is often prompted by artificially low wages and other costs
in the foreign countries where the work is now being performed. "Artificially,"
because wages and other costs aren't the function of free-market dynamics but
of, say, subsidies to firms or even slave or near-slave working populations who
are legally prevented from bargaining for wages and without lawful options
working for token sums. Of course, as noted already, the outsourcing can also
be the natural consequence of Draconian government regulations in the home
region, where firms and prospective employees are prohibited from determining their own terms of trade. Also, sometimes the impetus to send work abroad
results from the absence of legal protection of private property and personal
rights the protection of which would disallow dumping costs on the overseas
population in the form of disposing waste into the atmosphere. Of course, if the
choice between clean air and lower prices were available to many poor people,
they would probably chose the latter and be willing to put up with polluted
air. But when governments impose the policy by simply ignoring individual
rights, this is a moot point.

Many businesses have no compunction about taking advantage of such injustices, often to the detriment of prospective employees at home, where environmental restrictions – some of them quite sensible, such as bans on dumping
sludge, a form of unjust invasion, clearly – properly raise the cost of operating
a plant. (This is no different from property rights raising the cost of building
that the abuse of eminent domain allow some to circumvent.[62]

So what is one to say about outsourcing jobs overseas given such consider-
ations?

---

[62]Steve Greenhut, *Abuse of Power, How the government misuses eminent domain* (Santa Ana,
CA: Seven Locks Press, 2004).)

First, it is morally wrong and should be illegal to call upon government to play the tit-for-tat public policy game whereby some market distortion imposed abroad is then answered with a market distortion imposed at home; or some domestic injustice is met with further domestic injustice via government regulations. Someone must begin to clear the road to a free marketplace; and those of us discussing these matters in a particular region of the globe probably have a better – albeit often still minuscule – chance of influencing the citizens, politicians and bureaucrats within our reach than we of influencing those operating elsewhere.

Second, that people around the globe are being treated badly by their governments and that this abuse is sometimes exploited by various foreign companies does not provide grounds for continuing to treat people badly in one's own community, nor for imposing bans on free competition from foreigners. Whatever remedy is required for injustices anywhere, including those that harm persons in one's own country, cannot justify continuing and especially inaugurating injustices at home. The remedies must come another way; such is the imperative of morality and justice. (This kind of public policy is a version of tribalism whereby one punishes entire groups of people for the wrong that some of them have done.[63]

Some might retort by accusing proponents of the free-market alternative of lacking heart, of sticking their heads in the sand. But, in fact, champions of the free market are simply remaining loyal to a tried and true principle of sound political economy: implement freedom as far and wide as possible, and the results will be better and last longer, all things considered.

In other words, do not compromise on the principle of freedom of trade. None of us deserves to be penalized for the injustices perpetrated against others, by others.

9.   GLOBAL LABOR COMPETITION

The hate-filled outcry that jobs are "leaving the country" – however convoluted that concept really is – always calls to my mind the fact that many who voice it also posture as humanitarians. I have in mind the likes of Ralph Nader and Dick Gephardt, champions of the downtrodden and critics of big corporations. This refrain is most peculiar when coming from those on the Left who are ideologically committed to liberating the workers of the whole world, not just the workers of Detroit or Fresno. Indeed, if one is concerned about lack of jobs, it makes little sense to decry that condition only for Americans. Why

---

[63] Just what is wrong with such tribalist thinking is discussed at length in Tibor R. Machan, Classical *Individualism, The Supreme Importance of Each Human Being* (London, UK: Routledge, 1998).)

are Americans so special that they deserve jobs, but people around the globe, much worse off, do not?

There are ironies. The fact is, the more jobs we export, the better off the world becomes, which also means fewer people will wish to come here to find jobs – which has been the routine for about two centuries and which has upset some of the same folks – for example, Pat Buchanan – fretting about the loss of jobs and how "too many" immigrants are flooding our shores. If immigration is what you dislike, the greater availability of work abroad should delight you.

There is also something economically amiss with thinking of the creation of jobs abroad as a zero-sum game – as if those who live abroad never bought anything made by the folks here. We know darn well that everybody around the world watches American movies, listens to American music, drives American cars, and so forth. Are we to assume that this foreign demand does not redound to the benefit of American workers slogging away domestically in the companies purveying American culture and technology overseas? Suppose a moviemaker breaks even thanks only to foreign distribution of his film. With that foreign distribution, he is able to make his next movie. Without it, investors would have passed. Certainly the persons working on the set of that next movie have benefited from the success of the previous movie, success that would not have been possible without the overseas markets.

In fact the very idea of lining up all the American-made stuff on one side and all the foreign-made stuff on the other has become impossible, because it's all intermingled. Nearly everything is composed of parts that are made all over the place, with no way to tell sans special investigation where exactly they were made and who exactly made them. And if the socks or VCR are "made in America," what if they were made in another U.S. state – would the customers then become traitors to their own U.S. states, counties, or cities for buying the stuff not made precisely where they live?

If there is a sphere of human life that is in principle truly without borders, and ought to be as borderless as possible, it's commerce.[64] And that has been true over nearly all of human history. Commerce has, indeed, been responsible for much of the peaceful exploration of the globe, because of the motive to seek out new regions in which to buy and sell stuff.

Even the thought of trying to restrict the benefits of commerce to any particularly geographic area is galling, for no one can tell what exactly would need to be done to accomplish this, aside from throwing everybody in the neighborhood into a giant bubble which nothing may enter or leave. One sure would "create jobs" by this attempted constriction: the jobs of the police and military

---

[64]This, of course, is one of the central points of Adam Smith's classic, *The Wealth of Nations* (New York: Modern Library, 1993).

hired to engage in an utterly futile, hopeless effort to keep all the jobs local. But pointless busywork is not a productive form of employment.

Let us, however, consider a line of reasoning that might have led folks to reach conclusions other than those being advanced here. This line of reasoning – America-first in jobs – is very troublesome, considering, especially, that the U.S.A. is, perhaps more than any other country, populated with people who immigrated from other lands, or whose parents or grandparents did. I find it hard to charitably fathom how thoughtful Americans could begrudge foreigners their chance at a decent life. Sure, if they wish go out of their way to help some of their family members, friends and perhaps even neighbors on a voluntary, personal basis, that's understandable. But to try to erect "barriers to entry" is quite different – it's akin to shutting down a competing coffee shop across the street because one doesn't like customers preferring it to one's own, or preferring it to the shop of one's family or friends.

10. PROTECTIONISM REVISITED

My discussions of outsourcing, job losses, CEO pay, free trade policy and such, approached from a clearly normative political economic perspective – rather than one of positive economic science – have attracted their share of comments. After quoting an unvarnished endorsement, let us consider a much more critical missive:

> Sir, I have just finished reading your article on protectionism, and I feel that you are trivializing a very serious subject that is much deeper than you make it seem. I feel that you have very little respect for the people who toil with their hands, and you are obviously not one of those persons. I am Canadian, and I am not afraid to spend a couple of dollars extra on a purchase if it means keeping jobs in North America. I hope you are not including me when you refer to in voluntary slaves to the cost of making a purchase. What customers are you referring to anyway? Be cause the owners of big business will not be able to sell their product to the masses if they are all making three dollars a day! I wonder if you have researched the ultimate goals of the world trade organization because I found them quite frightening. When you are considered a resource and not a person in your country, it makes me want to puke. I hope you are not endorsing free trade, by the way, because it won't fly.
> The following does, I submit, address these concerns: ... Protectionism impoverishes millions abroad, in Third World countries, who could be competing with you and your North American pals but are prevented from doing so by those like you who believe they are virtuous when in fact they are steeped in the worst sort of chauvinism and prejudice in favor of members of your tribe. Those other human beings you so cavalierly dismiss from the human race have every right to compete with you and your fellows in North America. But no, you will not let them. Well, I have no respect for your wish to keep jobs where you live. What makes you and our neighbors so special that they ought to receive this illicit, nasty protection against those who are now disenfranchised? Not a thing.

This response underscores an aspect of protectionism that's too often neglected: how anti-humanitarian, in the usual sense of that term, protectionist positions tend to be, how they indulge in rank tribalism and chauvinism, despite any professions to the contrary. Suddenly the critics, with their altruistic excuses for various domestic public policies, lapse and exhibit their true colors. They start by construing free market capitalism ruthless, harsh, ungenerous but end by embracing ruthless, harsh and ungenerous public policies that dismiss the economic well being of millions who aren't part of their country (tribe?). So protectionism has nothing really to do with concern for the economic well-being of others but only with a crass, narrow vested interest, and with the refusal to adapt to changing circumstances. Only the notion that community life is inherently a Hobbesian war-of-all-against-all – of various groups against various other groups – could one begin to rationalize such lack of serious concern for the genuine well-being of all – something that only freedom can foster.

Some have argued that protectionism is on par with familial obligations according to which parents have special duties to help their children, for example. Yet the analogy fails because membership in a family is, as it were, "by invitation only" whereas being a fellow citizen is largely accidental. In any case, family ties commit one mainly to voluntary support, not to the establishment of barriers to entry and to abolishing the exit option. And, as the correspondent above suggests, to extend special consideration to fellow citizens is one thing, imposing trade restrictions on his or her behalf quite another.

11.   LOW WAGES FOR JOBS

One complaint often raised at meetings of the World Trade Organization in recent years echoes accusations that have been leveled at Nike Corporation, the entertainer Kathy Lee Gifford, Wal-Mart, Inc., and others who have employed workers abroad who charge far less for their labor than do workers in most Western countries. The critics charge that it is evil to pay so little for the work being provided in the developing world, and also unfair to those workers in the West who have fought long and hard to obtain better wages from their employers. Now, after all this struggle and the benefits workers in developed countries are finally reaping from it, companies are managing to escape the results by shipping operations to countries where wages are still low, where there is no organized "labor movement," and where other harms befall workers as well (for example, environmental destruction via the "costless" dumping of wastes, enabled by the lack of legal sanctions against it).

It is difficult to assess these charges without actually living in the regions of the globe where labor accepts the "cheap" wages, cheap at least in comparison to what labor gets paid in, say, Detroit, Paris or Toronto. After all, medical care is less expensive and less up to snuff in most such regions, as is entertainment, transportation, clothing, food, furniture and the rest. "Cheap" is relative.

In most regions of the world, the quality of life is lower than in "the West." Ironically, that is largely because in most regions of the world free trade had been either outlawed completely or curtailed severely by governments that have ruled there. Without free trade, labor cannot organize, wages cannot be bid up, the environment and, of course, the quality of goods and services suffer. It is hardly the fault of corporations that do business in these regions that they need not pay more for what they get.

To this observation, the critics respond that corporations ought to and should even be forced to pay more for the work. Kathy Lee has herself said she wishes the minimum wage were higher in Central America, where she does some business – as if she were stopped from raising wages unless the government forces her to do so. At any rate, there is a widespread sentiment, fueled by the likes of Ralph Nader and Michael Moore (the man responsible for such sanctimonious celluloid as "Roger and Me" and "The Big One"), that businessmen are obliged to seek out badly paid workers and raise their pay to what is confusedly called a "living wage."

This complaint does not square with the behavior of most people – not even with the behavior of most of those who advance it. Say we are in a grocery store and shop for some item, tea or chicken soup or soda pop. If we see that our preferred item comes in both an expensive and a cheap rendition, and we apprehend no other relevant difference between them, which do we purchase? At the mall, do we avoid stores where we cannot afford to buy goods and, instead, look for sales or good deals we can afford? When we shop for shoes, do we seek out the most expensive if we can find more reasonably priced ones that meet our needs? When one bids on a house or car, does one volunteer a higher price than the seller is asking? When going to a hair dresser or barber, does one look for the most expensive place to get what one is seeking to purchase? I believe the answers are uncontroversial here – mostly as shoppers, buyers we all want to obtain what we are after at the lowest possible price. Most people, in short, do not want to part with more rather than less of their wealth as they make their way about the marketplace. To waste money is to throw away opportunities – to save for a rainy day, to pay for something else. It is to behave irresponsibly.

People aren't in the marketplace primarily to be charitable: *and that goes for everyone, not just managers of multinational corporations.* If we shopped the way the protestors expect companies to shop, our families would be outraged by our lack of restraint or prudence. Even those firms that practice what is called socially responsible corporate management can only indulge this agenda in small measure, lest they become uncompetitive (although once they have made profits with comfortable margins, they can, of course, extend certain benefits to certain causes and groups they have chosen to help out.)

Just as charity begins at home, so does charitable wage negotiation. If you avoid the stores where goods are expensively priced, you are putting into motion a process that leads to the manufacturer of the goods sold there to seek out the cheaper rather than more expensive labor, cheaper rather than more expensive overhead, and cheaper rather than more expensive transportation. Those who buck this trend simply cannot attract customers and will, in time, go out of business. Cheaply paid labor will become unemployed labor.

In a free market there are better opportunities to improve one's bargaining power than there are in the regimented economies hailed by the protectionists and regulators. The latter rely on the non-existent omniscience of bureaucrats to set prices, wages, and production levels, with the result that the entire system is badly mismanaged.

Even such American academic sympathizers with socialism as the late John Kenneth Galbraith and Robert Heilbroner were obliged to admit that critics of the planned system like Ludwig von Mises and F. A. Hayek were vindicated when the Soviet Union's socialist economy collapsed.[65] Mises and Hayek had argued for decades that when people lack freedom to engage in local pricing, efficient communication of economic circumstances among the massive number of market agents is impossible. Coordination of their economic activities is radically impaired. Shortages and other forms of mismanagement will then be inevitable. (This is the so-called "calculation problem" of planned economies.)

Nor are heavily regulated economies – as opposed to outright centrally-planned ones – able to escape the brunt of this criticism. In such economies, too, bureaucrats pretend to know what people ought to want for themselves and under what terms. But this presumption also misfires and imposes costly wastes, all in the name of humanitarian sentiment that lacks economic sense. A lazy humanitarianism, at best.

What is fundamental to a prosperous economic system is freedom of trade among the participants. This means no slave labor, no restraints on trade by governments and criminals, no protectionism, no regulations imposed by the WTO or anybody else. The more freedom by way of strict protection of the

---

[65]For the late Robert Heilbroner's admission that Hayek and Mises were right, see his "After Communism," *The New Yorker*, September 10, 1990, p. 92. As to John Kenneth Galbraith, he was asked, in an interview published in *Ulisse*, Vol. 16, No. 145 (October, 1996) Alitalia's "in flight" magazine: "You spoke of the failure of socialism. Do you see this as a total failure, a counterproductive alternative?" He replies this way: "I'd make a distinction here. What failed was the entrepreneurial state, but it had some beneficial effect. I do not believe that there are any radical alternatives, but there are correctives. The only alternative socialism, that is the alternative to the market economy, has failed. The market system is here to stay."

right to private property and freedom of contract, the more abundant the economic opportunities will be for all concerned.

But freedom is not enough. Market agents must be alert to new ways of doing business, new technologies and the like. Complacency is deadly for economic prosperity. Sadly, however, many people believe short cuts can be taken and that the flexibility that economic progress requires both in their households and in the global economy can be preempted by instituting governmental protection against competition. And so they misguidedly clamor for protectionism.

What about child labor? Former President Clinton proudly signed a WTO agreement against it, but that could be no help to millions unable to enter some nice school (as Mr. Clinton dreamily envisioned) instead of going to work. For such kids, the alternative is often some kind of work versus some level of starvation. In many developing countries, sending a child to work can mean the difference between a reasonably solvent family and one on the brink of economic collapse.

In Hungary, as an eleven-year-old child, I worked as a baker's assistant, getting up at 4:30 a.m. and then leaving the bakery for school at 8 a.m., always pretty run down and in desperate need of sleep. But given that economically flattened society, the alternative was for me not to work at all – and for my family to eat much less. My mother already had to bring soup home from work every noon since we could not afford to buy any. Under such circumstances child labor is a blessing! Had it been forbidden, it would have been a back-breaker for our family. In societies where child labor is a "problem," it's not actually child labor that's the problem but the lack of adult economic opportunity.

The kind of agreement President Clinton signed in Seattle, on December 2, 1999,[66] may well have been a back-breaker for millions of families across the globe. In the name of resentment against corporations that make profits from the work of children, the president and his colleagues consigned a many children to hopelessness. If we really care about the well-being of people, all people all over the world, including kids, we have to shoot for much better than a "Dave"-level conception of how the world works.

12.   BIG BUSINESS ISN'T ALWAYS CAPITALIST

Genuine, honest capitalists work within the principles of the free market but, sadly, many corporations in fact violate those principles. No, I am not thinking here of bad management, which can bring a business to its knees but need by no means run afoul of free market ideals. What is at issue are those

---

[66]http://clinton4.nara.gov/WH/Work/childlabor.html

businesses, and there are a great many of them, that are managed not by way of the principles of the competitive market system but with the aid and support of coercive governments.

In Orange County, California, for example, the city officials of Cypress were recently being urged by Costco to use eminent domain powers to condemn the land owned by a nondenominational church, the Cottonwood Christian Center, and let the company build one of its stores there. Costco is a giant discount store that many members/customers who pay a yearly fee for membership like a great deal for its low prices and bulky discount sales. Costco's despicable conduct is but one case – there are thousands of other similar ones across the country, involving city officials colluding with big corporations that promise to generate sales and other tax revenues for cities and states, over and above what the threatened current owners of the properties pay. (In the Cypress case, the church pays no taxes, of course, which naturally irks the city politicians and bureaucrats who want something to carry on their parasitic practice of tax extortion. Fortunately, a court denied the city the eminent domain policy!)

It is too often believed by the critics and enemies of free market economics – that is, anti-capitalists – that the system is favored mainly by big corporations. Ralph Nader's relentless harangue against corporate commerce, as that of the adherents to the world-wide anti-globalization movement, creates this impression. Such critics are often unjust in their condemnations since many large corporations are managed by executives who are supportive of a *bona fide* free market and are committed to playing within the rules of such a system.

However, there are all too many completely unscrupulous managers of big firms who do not give a hoot about playing within those rules. These are the folks who run to government to obtain completely anti-competitive favors and who egg the state on to attack their competitors with feeble excuses about opposing monopolistic ways. That was the case with Netscape, which urged the government to break up Microsoft because, well, Microsoft played hardball in binding its less-desired products to others that were in high demand. Sure, this may have been irksome to Microsoft's competitors, and even to some customers, but there is nothing anti-market about such hardball practices. If I am a famous actor wanted by a studio, and I sign on only if my little brother also gets a part, so what? Sure, some other actor may be peeved, but that's how bargaining takes place – setting terms one likes and seeing whether those with whom one trades will accept them. Costco, in contrast, seems to be entirely oblivious to the fact that what it is urging the city of Cypress to perpetrate amounts (at least in terms of ethics or morality) to nothing less than theft. The company wants the city to steal the property of the church and let Costco build on it afterwards.

Those who have defended the institution of corporate commerce need not feel guilty, of course, since in principle small or large companies could function perfectly well without violating the principles of free trade and property rights. But it is scandalous that so many big businesses succumb to the temptation to get into bed with politicians and bureaucrats in a frontal assault on the rights of small property owners.

There is an irony in all this, when one considers that a great many critics of big corporations are also supporters of governmental regulation and management of various elements of the economy. They lament the power of big corporations, as against the lack of such power of smaller firms, seemingly favoring the latter but not the former. Yet many of these politicians and bureaucrats yield routinely to the urgings of big companies such as Costco – because doing so will enhance the revenue base of the political units involved – and by doing so, they are making it nearly impossible for small businesses to function securely. If the property of such small merchants and even churches – which is really a scary thought, is it not? – can be confiscated and given to large companies, how can one claim to favor small firms? Surely actions speak louder than mere political rhetoric. So, these folks, who deride big business yet approve of government regulations – and, especially, the corrupted version of eminent domain powers – are unequivocally aiding and abetting the (at least short-term) survival and flourishing of huge corporations as against small ones that are so clearly vulnerable to the collusive expropriation perpetrated by the former and their political and bureaucratic partners in "crime."

The moral of the story is that, while the free market is just and usually fair, many in business do not, by any stretch of the imagination, give it their support. Quite the contrary. In the end, though, they will regret this because, as politicians and bureaucrats can conspire against small business with big ones, so they can undo the big guys as well, should that suit their fancy. This is the phenomenon that economists have dubbed with the unfortunate phrase, "rent-seeking." It is unfortunate because, precisely meant, seeking rent is nothing insidious or ignoble – all apartment-house owners seek to be paid rent. Rent-seeking of the sort at issue here, however, is seeking to benefit from having funds gained from government that had been confiscated or gaining favors from government at the expense of others who must foot the bill for these favors.

Sadly, economics is widely taken to be a value-free science, so terms like "extortion," "theft," "robbery," and the like have been expunged from it. Instead "rent-seeking," "transfer payment" and "wealth redistribution" are being used, in part to disguise the ethical aspects of these undertakings by governments, ones that have, however, widespread support from champions whose morality runs counter to the ideas of individual rights, including private property and voluntary exchange. Once again, the most prominent champions of the free society and its market system have given up the capacity to provide their favorite system with a proper moral defense.

13.   WHY IS BIGGER NOT PERCEIVED TO BE BETTER?

Of course, bigger isn't always better, but perhaps it is safer and more effective and powerful, in some instances. Certainly many people believe this to be so, which is why they always want more members in whatever group to which they belong. United we stand, divided we fall, and the more who are united, the better. Leaders and champions of labor unions, auto clubs, AA and the AARP all think this way!

There is, however, an odd exception. When it comes to business, 'big' seems to bring on a great deal of wrath. Big businesses, big corporations, conglomerates, and such are routinely denounced for, well, just being big, or powerful or rich or some other thing. If you listen to Ralph Nader and company – and the company is much larger than his electoral support was in 2000, for obvious strategic reasons – it is big business that's responsible for every ill that's happening – pollution, unemployment, cheap labor, downsizing, housing developments that kill endangered species and destroy wetlands and the rest. The bigger, in this case, the worse, that seems to be the principle.

Now, why is this so? After all, there seem to be some rather evident advantages to big business. For one, a big, diversified corporation may be able to survive economic downturns more ably than some small mom-and-pop store. Just move traffic over a block, and the little shop goes bust, while big companies, with their numerous outlets and franchises, have a better chance of shifting costs and keeping their employees working. Then there is the fact that big companies can afford to do big deals, which sometimes involve some marvelous, huge and beneficial projects, like getting big planes off the ground, erecting a dam or luxury hotel, even contributing to various charities and causes. (What mom-and-pop store has managed lately to provide a university with a library or humanities center, or billions to fight African poverty and AIDS?)

Given these evident benefits produced by big business, what then is the trouble – that sometimes big companies do royal screw-ups? Yes, of course – people, be they alone or together, can make mistakes and even perpetrate outright wickedness. When there are a lot of people and they somehow get into the wrong frame of mind and collude, like OPEC does in spades (with, by the way, no major flack from the Ralph Naders among us), they can bring off some pretty nasty "business." Or just be mismanaged and go bust, as many huge companies have gone throughout the history of corporate commerce.

But big doesn't <u>have to be</u> wicked. It is indeed only those who have something against business itself, big or small, who would find its bigger versions to be especially prone to wickedness. And the reason is not all that difficult to detect, if one takes a look at most of the ruling ideas in both the East and West.

For one, the idea of being rich or getting wealthy hasn't gotten very good press in the respected literature of any civilization. Jesus, as I have noted before, got violent against money lenders, not the other sinners who defiled the sacred temple. Why did those guys deserve such ire while the others, who filled the temple no less than the lenders, got off scot-free? Then, also, the Bible tells us that a camel is likelier to fit through the eye of the needle than a rich man is to enter the kingdom of Heaven. Why – do the rich have some kind of sin gene? Or is there a bias here? Why, indeed, have money lenders gotten such a bad rap, so that in much of Europe only Jews became involved in banking and finance, for which they were then royally resented and horribly persecuted? What is wrong with lending out money for a fee? After all, one forgoes the use of the money while it's lent out and used by others.

Is it doubtful that business is getting an unfair rap? Just reconsider these "insights," already recounted in this work, from one of literature's prominent stars, Charles Baudelaire: "Commerce is satanic, because it is the basest and vilest form of egoism. The spirit of every business-man is completely depraved. Commerce is natural, therefore shameful." No, this is no isolated case. How does Arthur Miller, in *The Death of a Salesman*, depict the man whose profession is in sales? As a pathetic, shallow boor. Why?

Well, one way to look at this is that those not professionally involved in commerce tend to be rather jealous of the material success reaped by many who are. Writers, priests, artists, journalists and academicians (other than economists and business school professors) have a vested interest, generally, in peddling the idea that it is they whose ideas and way of life should be admired, with business looked upon as base and lowly. And why is this?

For one, these folks do not have the kind of clout that people in business do – one reason many of them look to government's taxing power to fund their endeavors. Business is sought out by ordinary folks – not so with conceptual artists or sophisticated playwrights.

Perhaps even more importantly, business is unabashedly natural, just as Baudelaire observes. And for that it must suffer, since the natural has generally taken an ethical back seat to the supernatural. And what within a person is supposed to reach out to the supernatural? It is one's soul or spirit, not the shameful material, natural self that goes shopping at the mall!

So while so many things that are big are praised (indeed, the bigger the better), big business tends to be demeaned, at least by those who are the opinion shapers in our culture. That is too bad, given how much good these folks do, both for themselves and for the rest of us.

Chapter 7

CORPORATIONS AND MORALITY

1. ENTERTAINMENT & BUSINESS

As I was channel surfing late one night, having just woken up from my second nap, I went past one broadcast channel on which I saw and heard the following sentence uttered by a young woman: "He was a businessman so he would do anything to turn a profit." I caught a glimpse of the name and it was Law & Order, Special Victim's Unit. Then I moved on.

But I could not shake the experience so I stopped searching for something to watch and began to reflect on what I just saw and heard. The sentence in question was extremely revealing. It gave a rather unambiguous characterization of how many in the entertainment industry understand business professionals.

Imagine if someone said on a program, "He was an artist so he would do anything to create something aesthetically worthwhile," or "She was a farmer so she would do anything to harvest her crop," or, yet again, "He was a professor so he would do anything to get his students to understand what they needed to know." By "anything" what is meant here, given the context, is even a heinous crime or something grossly unethical.

It is imaginable, of course, that an artist kidnaps some model so as to capture his or her image on canvas given that model's refusal to cooperate voluntarily. Or that a farmer might enslave a number of farm hands so as to get the crop harvested, given that he or she is short of funds to pay for their work. Or again that a professor would make use of something illicit, like the torture of some animal or even student, in order to teach a lesson.

Yet characters who are artists, farmers, or professors in television shows, movies or other fictional fares are rarely if ever portrayed that way. Rarely is it said of them that they would resort to anything to accomplish their professional objectives. It is well understood that they would instead adhere to ethical and legal standards. Artists are shown to get their work done, normally, without turning to crime, as are farmers, doctors, or teachers.

When it comes to how a great many in the entertainment industry conceive of people in business, there's a dramatic difference. Those who conduct business "would do anything to turn a profit." It is taken to be their nature to have no ethical or legal restraints, not unless they don't see how they could get away with it.

As a professor of business ethics this brings to mind the sadly but frequently heard notion that the very subject I teach is an oxymoron, a contradiction in terms. People in business simply cannot act ethically – business itself, like cheating at cards, is unethical. This notion is in part promulgated by those who produce entertainment fare around the country, even the world – screenwriters, novelists, dramatists, lyricists and so forth. And yet nothing can be further from the truth.

It is just as much of a false generalization about business that those working in the field will do anything to turn a profit as all those other generalizations I imagined before. Some, of course, will. But some health care professionals will do anything to accomplish their objectives, as we have been made aware recently from news reports about how at various hospitals they have been selling body parts without the authority to do so or engaging in various other forms of malpractice. (Just check out the news about what has been going on recently at the hospitals of UCLA and UCI, for example.) And there are professors who will utilize corrupt means by which to convey their message to their students, as we know from all the reports about biased instructions, the exploitation of research assistants, and so on and so forth.

In every profession there is the potential and there are some actual instances of unethical and illegal conduct, and this is, of course, true of business. But what seems undeniable is that those screenwriters, dramatists, novelists, and lyricists who churn out all the entertainment products that we see and read have it in mainly against people in business. For too many of these folks those in business simply "would do anything to turn a profit." Why? Not because there is evidence of disproportionate instances of unethical and illegal conduct by people in the profession. (If anything, considering the ubiquity of commerce in our society, there is not all that much immorality and illegality, not when one compares it to how politicians are doing.)

There is, rather, a prejudice about business, that's what explains it. There is a predisposition on the part of too many people among those giving us movies, television programs, pulp fiction, and drama to denigrate business. Even though these same folks are ever so eager to get their agents to make good deals for them, they regard deal making detestable, dirty.

The ultimate reason for this, I submit, is that when it comes to business, no one can deny that most people act in a self-interested fashion – they want to come out of a deal better off than they have gone in; they want to prosper from deals, not lose. They are not doing charity at the moment. And that means they cannot pretend to be altruistic as they carry on, not like farmers, artists or educators who can all make it seem they aren't in it to pursue some personal ambition but rather to serve some supposedly higher good or the public interest.

Which is, of course, bunk.

2. CORPORATIONS AND BAD EXTERNALITIES

In the controversial documentary, The Corporation, a good deal is made of the fact that corporations often produce what are called in economics "negative externalities." These are objectionable side effects of productive activities, best exemplified by pollution but not restricted to such obvious cases. The narrators of this program include among such externalities the cost of military actions they consider required to keep Middle Eastern oil flowing, the expense of building and maintaining public highways that are used for driving the vehicles that companies produce or use to transport their wares, etc.

There are many other allegedly negative features of corporate commerce the program identifies but let's just focus for a moment on negative externalities. In many cases of such externalities they can be internalized – companies can install equipment that treats waste so it doesn't become pollution. They can pay, via taxes or fees, for the military operations that may be required to keep secure the sources of oil. They are also paying for the roads on which they transport their products, via taxes, tolls, or fees of some kind.

Nor are corporations unique in producing negative externalities. (By the way, the program did not deal with the fact that business corporations also produce a good many positive externalities, such as information and, of course, the beneficial impact of the products and services people purchase from them.) We all produce bad side effects as we live our lives. Individuals, just as companies (of individuals), drive about and pour soot into the air mass. They dispose of waste routinely in such ways that it becomes a burden on others, too, as when public water treatment facilities are used to clean the water which has become contaminated by people.

In short, once some of the historical accidents have been dispensed with, business corporations turn out to be nothing more than people who have united to pursue certain economic objectives and in that pursuit produce some positive as well as negative side effects, just as we all do as we go about carrying out our various tasks in life. Only, of course, corporations act in ways that have bigger, more obvious effects than individuals produce in their disparate fashion. Such concentration of impact is easy prey for complaint, lament, and ascription of insidious conduct. And abuse. But in a free society, where no special privileges may be obtained from government by anyone or any group, a business corporation is no more than the united efforts of millions of people who have assigned the responsibility of professionally managing their investments for purposes of prosperity to a few people in such a way that it is these few people who are liable for any malfeasance, not the "silent partners." So long as this is publicly known to all who deal with the corporation, there is nothing amiss in the arrangement.

In The Corporation, for example, several comments are made about how such organizations are like killer sharks because they, like the sharks, have innate attributes to make them act aggressively. In other words, according to the producers of the program, corporations are innately driven to harm people with the bad side effects they produce. This isn't done intentionally, deliberately. No, that is just the nature of the beast, or so the producers contend, thus condemning them *en masse*.

In a way they are right but not as they would like to have us take it. Just as we, human individuals, go about our various tasks in life and produce bad side effects that we could dump on other people – I could take my trash and instead of paying a company to dispose of it or treat it, simply deposit it on my neighbor's lawn or some other place where others, not I, would be burdened by it – so companies often do go about their activities in ways that dump burdens on others. But they need not do so.

It is the function of a sound, just legal system to identify clearly enough each individual's and each corporation's legitimate sphere of authority, wherein acting with impunity would be unobjectionable but outside of which permission to act and dump would be required and would have to be paid for. We all, individuals and groups of them, need to know our sphere of sovereignty and this is part of what a legal order helps to identify and protect. Negative externalities need to be identified and no one may be empowered to inflict them on others.

Unlike the killer shark, which has no choice but to kill, individuals and companies of them do have a choice to perpetrate dumping or abstain from it. It may be difficult at times but it is not impossible. Contending that business corporations have it in their very nature to dump their negative externalities on unwilling others is to mischaracterize them quite unjustly.

3.   JOINING BUSINESS BASHERS

The UK magazine, *Marketing Week*, is a case in point: A rather well edited, comprehensive coverage of the marketing side of international business, it sadly, embraces the theme of most academic business ethics gurus. I am talking, once again, of CSR, the notion that the primary task of people in business is to act socially responsible. Managing a firm along these lines substitutes a doctrine of public service for taking good care of owners and investors. As if "the public" owned the firm!

As I noted in a recent column, this idea comes from those like Ralph Nader who hold that because some 500 years ago corporations had been creatures of governments – the crown established them, as it did virtually everything else that's important in a society – today they must still do their bidding. Which completely ignores the fact that monarchical rule was – and still is, where it's practiced – a fraud. No, kings, queens, and their gang do not own the realm. No, they aren't due anything from supposed subjects. No, they have no divinely anointed authority to run everything in society.

Kings and queens – and barons and dukes and the like – are posing as having special status among us all but it is high time this is thoroughly debunked. They are entitled to nothing special, least of all arranging, regimenting things in various countries around the globe. Nor is society, which is no entity but a bunch of various individuals.

And, thus, society isn't authorized to set up corporations either. That's what ordinary blokes like you and I and all the entrepreneurial types among us get to do once the ruse of monarchy and other statist myths has finally been exposed. And with that goes the idea that when people engage in commerce, their first duty is to serve the crown – or, as the Nader types would have it now, society.

Still, in criticizing a recent acquisition by perfume giant L'Oreal of The Body Shop, for 650 million pounds, the editor of *MarketingWeek*, Stuart Smith, lashed out at the former (3-23-06) on grounds that the purchase was an exercise in "unsentimental, unreconstructed capitalism." And he opined that "Sophisticated Western consumers are demanding more of trusted brands these days: their owners must also be sound on corporate social responsibility if they are to expect loyalty." And although "L'Oreal may have ceased animal experimentation in its R&D," Smith lamented that "it still uses ingredients that are animal tested."

So there is something anti-social in making sure by means of animal tests that ingredients of cosmetics are safe for human users? That's not even a matter of CSR but of rank kowtowing to the fanatical animal "rights" crowd which would dismiss human welfare so as to avoid offending the sentimentalists.

Well, with friends like editor Smith at *MarketingWeek*, the marketing arms of business don't need any enemies. They can just subject themselves to guilt-mongering from the likes of him and offer zero resistance to the business bashers in the academy.

It would be healthy to see some courage from those who cover the profession of business in the media, the likes of Stuart Smith; but, alas, it seems they aren't interested in the welfare of business. No, they appear to have joined with the scribblers in the halls of Ivy who are relentlessly trying to make of business a subservient group, one that, unlike those in other honorable professions, must do *pro bono* work 24/7.

This, sadly, is yet another sign that even in the West there is little clear understanding of capitalism and free markets. When the likes of Mr. Smith can bellyache about the selfishness of commerce, those in business may become tempted to put on the façade of altruism instead of carrying on with business as they should, conscientiously and with a clear eye to managing firms so as to make them prosper, to bring in profit rather than appeal to the business bashers.

4.   MUST CORPORATIONS BE STATIST?

It was Ralph Nader who advocated this idea back in the 1960s and 70s – that business corporations are actually arms of government, creatures of the state. Historically, of course, he was right that when monarchs ruled countries, they created business corporations. But they created nearly everything else, even churches, scientific projects, and the arts. That's because they ruled and the rest of us were their subjects. And they ruled often because it had been argued by their apologists that they owned the realm as a grant from God. This, the divine rights of kings, had been an influential doctrine and Nader in effect never gave it up!

After John Locke and, following him in more practical ways, the American founders overthrew the rationalizations for monarchy and laid the foundations for and established a relatively free country, governments lost their justification for any authority to impose rules that violate our basic rights. All sorts of institutions in society started to come under the management of the citizenry. It was they who then did society's work, created its businesses, its art, its churches and so forth.

Business corporations, too, began to be built from the bottom up – people started businesses and governments were merely registering their charters. This, at least, was the way things were supposed to happen until the government reasserted itself and grew and grew again, not just in size but, especially, in scope.

Today business corporations could be free but since everything else – universities, art museums, sports facilities, labor unions, you name it – is entangled with government, they too have become corrupted. So now a great deal of corporate commerce is sadly in cahoots with the state. Businesses receive government subsidies, bailouts, protection from competition, special favors of all kinds – but, of course, so do nearly all other special interest groups.

But this doesn't have to be. A business corporation could stand apart from government, and some in fact do so, if their owners and managers are principled enough and refuse to cave in to the temptation to get on the dole. No doubt this is difficult to do. Some will suffer competitively when they run a firm in a principled fashion. Just think, if various athletes are allowed to cheat, those who keep to the rules obviously will have a harder time keeping up. But some will insist on doing so because they do not want to profit at the expense of their souls, their integrity. But this is difficult to encourage when those who teach business ethics, not to mention political economy and philosophy, are so supportive of government meddling with the economy, including with corporate commerce.

Instead of sticking to principles, what most corporations do is hire a legal team and a substantial HR department that will help them navigate the treacherous waters of government regulation. The idea of doing the right thing then slowly metamorphoses into doing what is legally permitted. The very idea of business ethics evaporates. And the notion that corporate commerce must get into bed with government begins to be taken as a given.

This can only be combated by education, proselytizing, peer pressure, and so forth. Which is why the recent rise of free market and libertarian think tanks, web sites, newspapers and magazines, is so vital. It is these that may set the trend in the direction of a fully free society, as opposed to settling for the namby-pamby mixed economy with its innumerable semi-coercive institutions, including corporate commerce.

We can only hope that, in time, all institutions of society will be like journalism and churches, separated from government. Until then those who appreciate what is at stake, namely, the regime of individual liberty in all realms of social life, need to be ever so vigilant, which is after all the price of liberty.

5. FURTHER REFLECTIONS ON THE CORPORATION

On September 9th, 2004, *The Wall Street Journal* ran a sidebar titled "To Recruiters, Virtue is no Virtue." It reported that people who recruit for businesses do not really care whether students take courses in business ethics. "Virtue isn't high on the list of qualities corporate recruiters seek in students." This is what was supposed to be revealed in a *Wall Street Journal*/Harris Interactive survey.

However, the report and the survey that's its subject matter are quite unreliable. It turns out that instead of asking about business ethics, the survey asked about "corporate citizenship." No wonder most who were interviewed seemed skeptical about the relevance of "ethics" to business education – the concept of "corporate citizenship" isn't the same as ethics and so is misleading.

If one asks an educator whether ethics has anything to do with preparing educators for their profession, the answer will naturally be, "Yes, sure, of course it does, just as ethics has to do with preparing for and practicing any decent, *bona fide* profession." But if you ask whether education has anything to do with school or university citizenship, educators could well be quite baffled. Does that relate to whether educators ought to follow the law? Or be involved in politics? Does it mean one must be a good citizen of one's country so as to be a good educator, regardless of what the laws are or of what kind of politics are involved? What is meant, anyway, by such a loaded term as "corporate citizenship"? Business ethics is not about corporate citizenship, not if we consider the terms. Business is about guiding enterprises to prosper, toward profitability, and ethics is about doing this conscientiously, decently, guided by sound ethical concepts.

People in business take an oath of office, as it were, when they go to work in their profession and this commits them to be conscientious wealth producers. In the case of corporations, they sign up to care for the company's economic welfare, make it prosper, and fulfill its promise to produce conscientiously whatever it is that earns its revenue. That is where business ethics originates, from that promise, not unlike medical ethics comes from the doctor's promise to heal. Not that the ethics of human life in general do not apply, but even those do not commit one to treating one's profession as some kind of citizenship! They require one to be, among other things, honest, prudent, courageous, generous, and just.

Now if we asked people in business whether they take the promise involved in going into their profession seriously and whether schools of business ought to make clear that that indeed is the oath taken by business professionals, most would very likely answer, "Of course." But "corporate citizenship" is a term no one would think of – what does it mean, anyway?

Generally, students in business schools often face a very biased view of business ethics, for example, when they are asked about the social responsibility of corporate managers. Why "social" responsibility? Why not professional responsibility? After all, doctors, educators, scientists and artists, to name just a few other fields, do not talk about social responsibility. Sure, ethical business could include a social dimension, but whether it does should not be presumed. Nor should the decency and ethics of people in business be equated with the choice to do *pro bono* work. The main issue is whether business professionals fulfill their promise to work hard and conscientiously at the tasks they have assumed as they joined the profession.

Not that there is no debate about most of this. Some who reflect on the matter of the ethics of business professionals take it as given that such people are public servants, as would be those who work in the Department of Justice, police officers, or members of the various branches of the armed forces, but this is very dubious. Professionals do promise, in effect, to serve those who come to them for service, who hire them. But they are not committed to serve all who want what they have to offer. And they aren't public officials who must serve all citizens in society – all members of the public. If I haven't hired a broker, he or she owes me no advice. If I have no shares in a company, the managers aren't responsible to enhance my prosperity. But if I call the cops to help me cope with a crime, they owe me help simply because they are public servants.

Those who deny this adhere to what has come to be called the stakeholder – as opposed to shareholder – theory of the ethical responsibility of corporate managers. If you own a little shop next to a branch of a company, then if the managers decide that it would be economical to close this branch, they must, by this outlook, consider your interests as one of their priorities, not the shareholders'. Yet, this all rests on a view that denies a fundamental principle of business, namely, that trade must be voluntary. The company managers did not volunteer to serve the little shop next to the branch that's to be shut down. They did volunteer to manage the company for its owners.

At one time, of course, as Nader keeps stressing, all companies existed at the behest of the monarch and were, thus, public service institutions. Even the U.S. Constitution has some wording that suggests this: It treats commerce as something the free flow of which needs public support. In that the Constitution got it wrong – commerce, as religion or any other social projects, exists because members of society want it to exist, not because the government has decreed its value!

Consider, also, that few if any other professionals apart from business are expected to do *pro bono* work in order to earn moral standing. Companies are routinely expected to make huge contributions to charities, universities, international rescue missions. And they are expected to "give back" to their communities, as if they stole something from them! This is all utterly misguided and unfair, to boot.

In any case, whether business owes something to society and whether perhaps other professionals do as well are matters to be considered in a thorough exploration of professional and business ethics. It isn't to be laid down as axiomatic by some survey group and reported by The Wall Street Journal uncritically – as if nothing problematic were contained in the finding that business recruiters don't much care about whether students in business schools take courses in "corporate citizenship." Perhaps they shouldn't. Perhaps recruiters and students really ought to care about being decent professionals in business, period.

6.   BUSINESS ETHICS DISTORTIONS

Ethics is an ancient discipline, mostly tackled by philosophers. It addresses the issue of how human beings should choose to live, what standards should guide them in deciding what conduct is right, what is wrong. And it concentrates mainly on broad principles or virtues – honesty, generosity, temperance, courage, moderation, prudence, and so forth. Philosophers tend to argue about the exactly ranking of these principles or virtues, as well as about whether ethics is possible at all.

There has always been some interest on the part of certain philosophers in the application of ethics to specific areas of human life – parenting, farming, medicine, business, engineering, and so forth. For some years, however, the study of business affairs was completely taken over by economics, which is deemed a social science. Thus ethics had been set aside where business was being investigated – it was assumed, largely, that what happens in commerce and business goes on as a kind of natural process, driven by the innate human impulse to prosper – in other words, the profit motive.

In time, however, it became evident that business, like other special areas of human concern like medicine or law, also needed to be studied with an eye to its special ethical dimensions. That gave rise to the currently widespread and even fashionable academic field of business ethics.

Apart from cynics, who say "business ethics" is an oxymoron, those who study the field tend to bring to it the most prominent ethical theories within the philosophical community. Those mainly include utilitarianism – strive to promote the general welfare – and altruism – serve your fellow human beings first and foremost. Yet, oddly, this is not what those who study the special ethical dimensions of, say, art or science or even medicine focus on.

In these other professions it is widely understood that the ethical guidelines arise from the purpose that's to be served by the profession. So that education, for example, should generally be guided by the goal it serves – imparting knowledge and understanding to students. That purpose, of course, must be pursued without doing violence to ordinary ethical principles or virtues. So educators may not ignore honesty and generosity and prudence as they do their work. But their special purpose is to teach.

For the profession of business, however, this idea has been undermined. Instead of acknowledging that those in the profession ought to strive to produce wealth – heed the bottom line, for which they are hired by the owners of firms, investors, shareholders, and so forth – many teachers of business ethics have embraced the doctrine of Corporate Social Responsibility. This basically holds that the primary goal of those in business must be to advance the social or common good, never mind their professional obligations to those who have hired them, their clients.

Now business is unabashedly committed to promoting prosperity, to seeking a profit, and this goal has irked a great many people, especially many philosophers. Too many of them have embraced, instead, the ethical view that our actions should serve humanity or other people, not our own well-being or success in life. So unlike what seem more like service professions – thus appearing mainly to be helpful – business is more directly aimed to advancing the benefits of the owners.

Of course, in medicine this holds as well – doctors and health professionals are hired to serve the well being of their patients or clients, not of society or someone down the street. So there's nothing off about an ethical perspective in which the emphasis is on benefiting clients. But with health this seems less objectionable than with wealth, for a variety of reasons. The pursuit of prosperity has always been problematic among philosophers and theologians, starting with Socrates and Christ all the way to today's teachers in the field.

Nonetheless, the idea that business must be aimed to benefit society is highly dubious. It comes from the historical accident that it was the monarch who initially set up business corporations. But that's because it used to be the monarch who set up everything – religion, science, the arts, you name it.

Since monarchies have been discredited as fraudulent – no one is really appointed by God to run other people's lives, to own and care for the realm – businesses, too, are primarily private enterprises, not state projects. And this is where the myth of CSR breaks down. Corporate managers have as their goal to serve their owners, not society, humanity, the nation, or anything of that sort. This doesn't mean those in business have no other responsibilities than to enrich the folks who hired them. But while on the job, that's mainly what they ought to be doing.

Chapter 8

WEALTH CARE AND MORE

1.   ALTRUISM IN PERSPECTIVE

When it comes to morality or ethics, most people champion altruism. This is the view that, when one acts, one must have other people's well being as one's prime purpose, one's priority. Without this, one is a selfish cad or, at best, amoral. As one philosopher specializing in moral theories, tells us, "'Altruism' [is] *assuming* a duty to relieve the distress and promote the happiness of our fellows .... Altruism is to ... maintain quite simply that a man may and should discount altogether his own pleasure or happiness as such when he is deciding what course of action to pursue."[67]

Yet most of us carry on, day to day, as if it is our own well-being that matters to us first and foremost. Of course, this can include our family, friends, or some organizations (such as our place of work or a team or club to which we belong). In each of these cases, however, we are very closely involved, and doing what benefits our family, friends and organizations pretty much amounts to doing what benefits ourselves or, at least, our own purposes.

So it looks like we do not do as many of us proclaim or are told. "Be unselfish," is our message, but "Do what is in my best interest," is what we actually follow. Are we really such hypocrites? Do we lead such a life of duplicity? Or might there be some kind of misunderstanding afoot here?

When one thinks it over, it looks like the altruism we champion is actually not one promoting unselfishness but rather of extended selfishness. Here is a case in point: A mother runs into a burning house to rescue her child. She perishes in the attempt. We regard her as unselfish, a martyr, willing to sacrifice herself for the sake of her child. Yet, the mother chose to have and rear the child, so it is not true that her action was unrelated to her own objectives in life. Indeed, she was serving what might best be construed as her extended self. She was selfish in the broad sense of what one's self amounts to, namely, a network of chosen concerns and relationships.

Or consider how teammates often appear to be unselfish when they forgo the chance to attempt to score and let someone else do so. Is this really unselfishness or is it team work that one has chosen to be part of, for one's own

---

[67]W. G. Maclagan, "Self and Others: A Defense of Altruism," *Philosophical Quarterly* 4 (1954): 109–127.

purpose or agenda? If the latter, is it really altruistic? Answering that question would require close scrutiny, not some vague general perspective.

Even when we talk about total strangers, we often understand their actions in the light of an implicit commitment to other people – neighbors, colleagues, fellow citizens. We are part of many, many communities and as we join them, whether suddenly or gradually, their members and the concerns of those members become ours, as well. So when we show loyalty to these, we are not altruistic or unselfish, but are seeing ourselves broadly. We identify our own well-being with theirs, just as a mother does her child's with hers.

One problem we find is that many people who make such commitments then fail to remain loyal to them. They neglect their commitments – as when a teammate hogs the ball and fails to live up to his or her commitment to help the team win. Or consider a situation where a member of the family who has in effect taken an oath to work to advance the family's well being decides to act only for his or her own private benefit. We often misguidedly consider this selfishness. In fact, it may be a lack of the kind of self-love that Aristotle, the great ancient Greek philosopher, identified. As some economists would put it, we all have a positive interdependent utility function: Our happiness or success in life depends on others being happy or succeeding, as well. This explains, they would argue, why women do not rush into every burning building to save the children there, but mostly only if their own child is at risk.

Sadly, there is a prominent modern understanding of the nature of the human self that is at fault here. By this account (promoted by Thomas Hobbes, the 16th Century English philosopher), the self is but a bundle of desires and passions, concerned with no more than gaining power. And that has come to mean selfishness, rather than Aristotle's idea of intelligent, gregarious self-love.

Once Aristotle's idea is appreciated and gains some currency again, the conflict between self and others no longer holds sway. Others – at least some significant ones – are indeed part of ourselves or, at least, the interest of ourselves. That would explain why we complain when some people fail to be helpful, caring and thoughtful – because, in fact, they are not doing a good job of taking care of themselves, as broadly interpreted. They are, in effect, going back on their word.

Indeed, altruism proper, the primary devotion to others in one's life, is impossible to practice and leaves us with perpetual guilt. It also makes little sense: If you work mainly to benefit others, and they work mainly to benefit yet others, and so on and so on, no one will ever benefit at all, except for those who are immoral and decide to keep some of those benefits for themselves. The pure altruism of ethical theory is impossible to practice, while the broadly understood self-love clearly is practicable, and can give one a reasonable involvement with the well being of significant and even remote others.

Why is this relevant here? Simply because, quite often, capitalism and commerce are bashed for catering to selfishness, the pursuit of self-interest. While that idea is a bit confusing in the hands of economists – who mostly mean only that under a free-market economy people can pursue their own goals, whatever those may be – it also means that yes, indeed, under capitalism people may freely pursue goals that are in their own best interest, and that will in fact benefit them, first and foremost.

Now unless we understand by such selfishness or self-interest something morally unobjectionable, something that's actually quite proper, the system could be faulted for this. But when we see that selfishness, properly understood, means actually striving to make the most of one's life as a human being, and that it is in this context that economic pursuits must be understood, then there's nothing wrong with the fact that capitalism makes selfishness possible, or even encourages it. As a corrective to guiding commerce and business via altruism, it will be best to take a closer look at how Aristotle's ethics can be updated for that purpose.

2.   PHILOSOPHERS AND ETHICS

With the possible exception of Immanuel Kant, no one has influenced philosophical thinking about ethics or morality as much as Aristotle. At first, Europeans tended to follow the guidance of Socrates and Plato in how they saw the world and how they conceived of human excellence via the shaping of Christianity by Plotinus (namely, in idealistic ways, in urging us all to aim for the impossible dream of perfection). During the thirteenth century, however, Aristotle reemerged as the most prominent thinker to anchor Christian thought (via the works of St. Thomas Aquinas), and prudence once again became prominent as a human virtue.

This is significant for any assessment of the moral standing of business; the ways in which Christianity and other world views have encouraged understandings of commerce has made a considerable difference in how commerce came to be regarded. It is in part because of the influence of such views that, even in our time, with business enjoying global presence and prominence, many people still cannot resist the temptation to say that the very idea of 'business ethics' is an oxymoron, and why so many people in the arts and humanities find commerce utterly distasteful.

Consider, again, Charles Baudelaire's earlier quoted comment that "commerce is satanic, because it is the basest and vilest form of egoism."[68] Consider, as well, Arthur Miller's attitude, when he noted: "His was a salesman's

---

[68]Op. cit., *Intimate Journals*, p. 89.

profession, if one may describe such dignified slavery as a profession."[69] Also, consider that "for profit," which is what business is about, has acquired negative connotations, as compared to "for the public interest." "Commercialism" is also a term of denigration. It is probably no accident that Karl Marx, a recent nemesis of bourgeois values, drew on some of the ideas of Aristotle concerning wealth and exchange.

In particular, Plato found commerce to be lowly, and Aristotle did not think all that highly of it, either, especially retail trade, one of commerce's most prominent manifestations in contemporary life. Aristotle was friendlier to commerce than Plato, but his views suggest that he did not believe we could live a good human life by making a career of business. Aristotle supports the institution of private property rights as a far more efficient way of allocating resources, including labor, than alternatives such as Plato's anticipation of communism. Given that the right to private property is basic to the conduct of trade, Aristotle can be taken to be far more supportive of business than was Plato.[70]

Why did Aristotle think commerce or retail trade was a second rate activity? Why, by implication, would those following him, as well as others with whose ideas his became mixed, regard business as an inferior profession – compared, say, to philosophy, science, politics or medicine?

It will be useful to consider this because certain subtle errors appear to have tilted an otherwise clear-thinking Aristotle in the direction of demeaning commerce and business. With those errors repaired, Aristotle's guidance could, in fact, be the best approach to understanding business and to developing a successful concept of business ethics. It is, after all, Aristotle who regarded prudence as a prominent moral virtue. Therefore, if being conscientious about oneself and one's own flourishing is the hallmark of prudence, then commerce and the profession of business could well be supported by this virtue.[71] It all depends, however, on how one understands the human self toward which one ought to exercise good care.

3.   ARISTOTLE'S OVERLY INTELLECTUALIZED ETHICS

In the *Nicomachean Ethics,* Aristotle investigates the nature of happiness. In the following passage, he gives a good summary of his ideas:

---

[69] Arthur Miller, "In Memoriam," *The New Yorker*, 25 December 1995 & 1 January 1996. One may wonder whether Miller collected pay for his work, royalties and such, and whether Marx, too, had mercenary goals.

[70] See, Tibor R. Machan, *The Right to Private Property* (Stanford, Calif.: Hoover Institution Press, 2002).

[71] See Douglas J. Den Uyl, *The Virtue of Prudence* (New York: Peter Lang, 1991).

> If happiness is activity in accordance with excellence, it is reasonable that it should be in accordance with the highest excellence; and this will be that of the best thing in us. Whether it be intellect or something else that is this element which is thought to be our natural ruler and guide and to take thought of things noble and divine element in us, the activity of this in accordance with its proper excellence will be complete happiness. That this activity is contemplative we have already said.[72]

To this he adds:

> [T]his activity is the best (since not only is intellect the best thing in us, but the objects of intellect are the best knowable objects); and, secondly, it is the most continuous, since we can contemplate truth more continuously than we can *do* anything.[73]

Aristotle thinks so highly of reason because it is the means by which the best knowable objects are apprehended. This appears to hark back to Plato's idea that reason is best because it grasps the forms of things. In Aristotle's view, we must deploy the several senses in order to form the abstractions that apprehend principles and theories and the forms of things. According to Aristotle, then, the happiest life is contemplative. Moreover, the virtues that enhance such a life must then be the most important virtues. Whatever they are, a morally or ethically good person will have to practice them.

Aristotle appears to have believed that contemplation, the fully engaged activity of the human reason or intellect, is the highest moral virtue. This, at least, has been a common understanding of his teaching and is consistent with the Socratic tradition that the unexamined life is not worth living. Along with this teaching seems to have gone the implication that craftsmanship, productivity, or making does not amount to the sort of practice that can be highly virtuous or noble. Accordingly, persons who are engaged in making things, including making wealth, such as traders or merchants, do not have good a chance of living morally excellent lives. The exception, for Aristotle, seems to be statesmen or political leaders who, though not engaged primarily in contemplation, practice certain virtues such as valor and magnanimity, and are thus capable of leading noble lives.

Let us turn to Aristotle's position or, perhaps more accurately, the legacy of that position. Arguably Aristotle focuses on the intellect to the neglect of other, equally vital human capacities, and thus concludes that a happy life could only be a contemplative life. This is misguided. It has misled many people who were taught by Aristotle and some of his prominent interpreters to think that the correct understanding of an ethical life favors, primarily, the activity of intellectual contemplation. This strongly suggests that anyone pursuing a profession in commerce or business, much less retail trade, cannot attain moral excellence.

---

[72] Aristotle, *Nicomachean Ethics* in *The Basic Works*, ed., Richard McKeon (New York: Random House, 1941), bk X, ch. 7; 1177^{a}11–19; p. 1104.

[73] Ibid.

Actually, there are different ways Aristotle characterizes what he takes to be the most noble, ethically worthwhile human life. In his *Rhetoric*, he tells us that altruistic conduct, not contemplation, is the noblest type of conduct:

> "Again, those actions are noble for which the reward is simply honour, or honour more than money. So are those in which a man aims at something desirable for some one else's sake; actions good absolutely, such as those a man does for his country without thinking of himself; actions good in their own nature; actions that are not good simply for the individual, since individual interests are selfish. [1367a] Noble also are those actions whose advantage may be enjoyed after death, as opposed to those whose advantage is enjoyed during one's lifetime: for the latter are more likely to be for one's own sake only. Also, all actions done for the sake of others, since less than other actions are done for one's own sake; and all successes which benefit others and not oneself; and services done to one's benefactors, for this is just; and good deeds generally, since they are not directed to one's own profit."[74]

Aristotle's focus on contemplation as the most excellent virtue has even led him and many others who have merged it with various strands of thought, mostly drawn from Christian theology, to view commerce, among other human endeavors, as lowly and ignoble.[75] Another such endeavor is human sexuality which, like commerce, is treated in a schizophrenic fashion in much of Western culture: we tend both to prize and to demean it. Consider George Kennan on human sexuality:

> "There is no getting around it: we have to do here with a
> compulsion we share with the lowest and least attractive
> of the mammalian and reptile species. It invites most
> handsomely, and very often deserves, the ridicule, the
> furtive curiosity, and the commercial exploitation it
> receives. To highly sensitive people, it can become a
> never-ending source of embarrassment and humiliation,
> of pain to its immediate victims and to others, of
> misunderstandings, shame, and remorse all around.
> Not for nothing do the resulting tragedies dominate so
> much of realistic as well as of romantic literature. Not
> for nothing has this urge earned the prominent place it
> takes in the religious rites of confession and prayers for
> forgiveness."

---

[74]Ibid., bk. 1, ch. 9; 1366^{b}34–1367^{a}7; p. 1355.

[75]The irony does not escape some commentators that Aristotle, a supreme contemplator himself, would regard contemplation as the highest stage of moral excellence, just as Plato had regarded pure reason as the road to the highest good that human beings can achieve.

There is, in short, no escaping it: the sexual urge, the crude expression of nature's demand for the proliferation of the species, enriching, confusing, and tragedizing the human predicament as it does at every turn, must be regarded as a signal imperfection in man's equipment to lead life in the civilized context. It cannot be expected to be otherwise at any time in the foreseeable future.[76]

3.1.   The Superiority of Intellect

Aristotle tells us that intellectual life embodies what is true human excellence and, thus, counts as the morally or ethically highest form of life:

> "So if among the excellent actions political and military actions are distinguished by mobility and greatness, and these are unleisurely and aim at an end and are not desirable for their own sake, but the activity of intellect, which is contemplative, seems both to be superior in worth and to aim at no end beyond itself, and to have its pleasure proper to itself (and this augments the activity). And the self-sufficiency, leisureliness, unweariedness (so far as this is possible for man), and all the other attributes ascribed to the blessed man are evidently those connected with this activity, it follows that this will be the complete happiness of man, if it be allowed a complete term of life (for none of the attributes of happiness is *in*complete)."[77]

We can see from this that, for Aristotle, a contemplative life is a theoretical life. He links such a life to the knowledge of principles, as in philosophy and the sciences. Thus we see that Aristotle is here close to Plato's intellectualism, although Plato's dualism gives stronger support to this stance.

Perhaps what Aristotle thinks is indeed right, precisely as has been believed by many who have urged us all to embrace the mental or spiritual as the highest form of life. Certainly in Western cultures the idea has had considerable impact. The Nobel Prize is given to theoreticians: educators are honored far above, say, merchants, playwrights far above actors and pure mathematicians far above those dealing with applied math. Priests and nuns in the Roman Catholic church enjoy both official and unofficial respect and status. In the case of the writings of Western thinkers, their own profession, namely creative writing on abstract subjects, is more highly honored than, say, farming or business. There are some philosophers who believe differently, but the focus here is on dominant trends. Even in Marxism, despite the high regard in which the workers, largely physical laborers, are held, the culmination of humanity's development promises to usher in the intellectual-spiritual lifestyle wherein menial labor will have been taken over by machines, thereby freeing men and women to enjoy what could easily be taken to be a philosophic life.

---

[76]George F. Kennan, *Man, The Cracked Vessel* (New York: W. W. Norton, 1993), pp. 19–20.

[77]Aristotle, op. cit., bk. X, ch. 7; 1177^{b}18–25; p. 1105.

Yet Aristotle also understands that human beings are rational animals, which is their nature. This means everyone, to be human, must be both an animal and a rational, thinking being. Given Aristotle's naturalism, this suggests that even though he believes intellect to be the right candidate for what should be our natural ruler, Aristotle should make some room here for non-intellectual elements, given that they too are part of our nature. It looks like Aristotle is caught in a mistake: he does not pick what is natural to human beings, what it is that we all must be to be human; rather, he picks what serves as our distinctive essence, what it is about our nature that is distinctive, as the proper standard of human goodness. Arguably, this perpetuates the normative implications of the dualism that his mentor, Plato, appears to have advocated. This is so, despite the fact that Aristotle rejects metaphysical dualism in the bulk of his philosophy.

For Plato, ethical rationalism or intellectualism made sense since, at least by one common interpretation of his views, he believed that our intellect is uniquely in touch with a superior, perfect, immaterial, even supernatural realm of reality. Aristotle's ontology, however, ill equips him to place one part of our nature above others. Aristotle is a monist and sees all of reality or nature as one, undivided into higher and lower parts.

Aristotle's mistake, coupled with Plato's dualism and its extensions via Plotinus and Christianity, has helped perpetuate an idea of commerce, and the profession of business, that has been unwise and unjust. Unwisely, it promotes the view that when we try to prosper, as we conduct commerce and take up the profession of business, we lack serious moral standing. In contrast, people in education, science, the arts, and other professions tend to receive undue respect, so much so that even the law accords them preferential treatment, leaving them free to do what those in the business professions are not. It is unjust because it has roundly consigned us, as we engage in commerce, especially business professionals, to a subordinate social and moral status.

Some people point out that there is plenty of respect shown to business in our culture and there is, indeed, of a certain sort. Business is shown a kind of admiration for savvy, cleverness, and shrewdness. Yet moral credit comes to business mostly from *pro bono* work, and from bequeathing large sums to universities, museums, libraries, and other non-business institutions.[78]

No claim is made here that Aristotle was a dualist or that his intellectualism puts a wedge between mind and body in the fashion encouraged by Plato and made prominent in many religions, including Christianity. Indeed, had it been for Aristotle alone, without the subsequent mixing of his views with Thomistic Christianity and scholasticism, the place of commerce in human social life might well have been far more respectable than it became, even after

---

[78] See, op cit., Machan and Chesher, *The Business of Commerce.*

Plato's influence had waned. Aristotelianism, however, was widely combined with Thomism and thus emerged in a dualist rendition. This is what turned so much of early modern philosophy against him or his contaminated rendition concerning, for example, the nature of natures.

A revival of Aristotle's original philosophical method, along with some modification of the substance of his thought (for example, regarding slavery, the nature of women, and essentialism versus naturalism) would serve us well in moral philosophy, in business ethics and in life itself. This is especially so in light of the unfortunate and even tragic results of the promulgation of Kantian views of morality, which have tended to render the virtue of prudence morally irrelevant, given that it cannot be construed as impartial and disinterested by any stretch of the imagination, any more than profit seeking can be so construed.

With the reconsideration and renewed appreciation of the Aristotelian approach to morality, minus its misleading ties to the meta-ethics of essentialism as distinct from naturalism, professions that are supposed to enhance our lives need not be seen as resting on various involuntary tendencies. They need not rely on a supposed drive for self-preservation and self-aggrandizement (a drive that later was transformed into a supposedly innate profit-motive and the *homo economicus* thesis about people as utility-maximizers), but can be understood as having a worthwhile, morally virtuous, prudential purpose.

BIBLIOGRAPHY

Arblaster, A. (1984) *The Rise and Decline of Western Liberalism* (Oxford: Basil Blackwell).

Arrow, K. J. (1981) "Two cheers for government regulation", *Harper's,* March, pp. 18–22.

Becker, Gary, (1976) *The Economic Approach to Human Behavior* (Chicago: University of Chicago Press).

Bethell, Tom (1998), *The noblest triumph: Property and prosperity through the ages* (New York: St. Martin's Press).

Buchanan, James, and Tullock, G. (1962) *The Calculus of Consent* (Ann Arbor: University of Michigan Press).

Conway, D. (1987) *A Farewell to Marx* (New York: Penguin).

Etzioni, Amitai, *The Spirit of Community* (New York: Crown, 1993).

Friedman, M. (1953a) *Essays in Positive Economics* (Chicago: University of Chicago Press).

——. (1962) *Capitalism and Freedom* (Chicago: University of Chicago Press).

——. (1976) "The line we dare not cross", *Encounter*, November, pp. 8–14.

Galbraith, J. K. (1973) *The Affluent Society,* 3rd ed., (Boston: Houghton Mifflin).

Gordon, B. (1975) *Economic Analysis Before Adam Smith* (New York: Barnes & Noble).

Hayek, F. A. (1960) *The Constitution of Liberty* (Chicago: University of Chicago Press).

Hessen, R. (1979) *In Defense of the Corporation* (Stanford: Hoover Institution Press).

Kirzner, I. M. (1973) *Competition and entrepreneurship* (Chicago, University of Chicago Press).

Machan, T. R. (1990) *Capitalism and Individualism* (New York: St. Martin's Press).

Machan, T. R. & James E. Chesher (2003). *A Primer on Business Ethics* (Lanham, MD: Rowman & Littlefield).

Marx, K. (1977) *Selected Writings,* ed. by D. McLellan (London: Oxford University Press).

McCloskey, D. N. (1985) *The Rhetoric of Economics* (Madison: University of Wisconsin Press).

McKenzie, R. (1983) *The Limits of Economics Science,* (Boston: Kluwer-Nijhoff).

Metcalfe, J. S. (1998) *Evolutionary economics and creative destruction* (London: Routledge).

Mill, J. S. (1871) *Principles of Political Economy with Some of its Applications to Social Philosophy,* 7th edition, (New York: D. Appleton).

Mises, L. von (1949) *Human Action,* New Haven: Yale University Press.

Mishan, E. J. (1986) "Fact, faith, and myth: Changing concepts of the free market," *Encounter,* November, pp. 65–7.

Morris, C. (1972) *The Discovery of the Individual 1050–1200* (New York: Harper & Row).

Nader, R., Green, M. J. and Seligman, J. (1976) *Constitutionalizing the Corporation: The case for federal charting the giant corporations* (Washington, DC: Corporate Accountability Research Group).

Novak, M. (1979) *Capitalism and socialism: A theological inquiry* (Washington: American Enterprise Institute for Public Policy Research).

Pipes, Richard, (1999) *Property and freedom* (New York: Alfred A. Knopf).

Radnitzsky, G. and Bernholz, P. (1987) *Economic Imperialism* (New York: Paragon House).

Rawls, J. (1971) *A Theory of Justice* (Cambridge: Harvard University Press).

Rothbard, Murray, N. (1995) *An Austrian Perspective on the History of Economic Thought* (Aldershot, Hants, England; Brookfield, Vt: Edward Elgar Publishers).

Sen, A. K. (2001) *Development as freedom* (Oxford: Oxford University Press).

Smith, Adam, (1776) *An Inquiry into the Nature and Causes of the Wealth of Nations* (Dublin, Whitestone).

Sowell, T. (1985) *Marxism* (New York: William Morrow & Co.).

Stigler, G. (1982) *The Economist as Preacher, and Other Essays* (Chicago: University of Chicago Press).

Schwartz, Jeffrey M., and Sharon Begley, (2002) *The Mind & The Brain* (New York: Regan-Books).

Taylor, Charles "Atomism," (1985). *Philosophy and the Human Sciences* (Cambridge: Cambridge University Press).

Tawney, R. H. (1926) *Religion and the Rise of Capitalism: A historical study* (New York: Harcourt, Brace & Co.).

Von Mises, (1949) *Human Action* (New Haven: Yale University Press).

Walker, M. ed., (1988) *Freedom, Democracy, and Economic Welfare* (Vancouver: Fraser Institute).

Zakaria, Fareed (2003) *The future of freedom: Illiberal democracy at home and abroad* (New York: W. W. Norton & Co).

Index

lynch mobs 30

Machan, Tibor 2n, 3n, 5n, 56n, 58n, 61n,
  62n, 83n, 84n, 86n, 97n, 124n, 128n
Maclagan, W. G. 121n
Mafia 95
majority rule 65
malpractice 6, 71, 88, 110
Mamet, David 17
Mandeville, Bernard 9
manipulate 41, 75
Mao 30
market socialism *see* socialism, market
Marketing Week 112, 113
Martin, Steve 27
Marx, Karl 11, 12, 20, 22, 30, 32, 49, 51,
  66, 66n, 67, 86, 86n, 87, 124, 124n
Marxism 51, 86, 127
Marxist(s) 12, 40, 45, 51, 55
materialism 49
McCloskey, D. N. 14
mercantilism 7, 8, 81, 88
Metcalfe, J. S. 10
Microsoft 72, 104
Miller, Arthur 17, 107, 123, 124n
Mises, Ludwig *see* von Mises
monarchies 53, 119
monarchy 23, 113, 114
monopoly 73
Moore, Michael 101
Moorehouse, John C. 4
Muslim(s) 48, 49

Nader, Ralph 62n, 79, 92, 97, 101, 104,
  106, 112, 113, 114, 117
Nagel, Thomas 5, 6, 6n
Nanny State 82
National Public Radio 83
nationalism 25, 29
native Americans *see* Indians
natural liberty 66
natural rights 10, 58
Nazism 45
Nazis 20
negative externalities 111, 112
Netscape 104
Nevada 54, 92
New Hampshire 83
New York Times 39, 94
Newtonian physics 41

Nicomachean ethics *see* ethics,
  Nicomachean
Nightly News 89–90
Nike 100
Nisbet, Robert 66, 66n
Nobel Prize 16n, 18, 57, 127
normative economics 13
Novak, Michael 10
Nozick, Robert 42, 43

Objectivism 47
Olympic Games 25, 27, 30, 31
"one-size-fits-all" 1, 30, 76, 87n
OPEC 106
open society 37, 40, 43
Orange County 104
outsourcing 29, 94, 96, 99

Pareto optimality 4
Pareto, Vilfredo 10
patriotism 29
paternalistic laws 3
Peace Corps 72
Peltzman, Sam 62n
Pierson, N. G. 55n
Pipes, Richard 10
Plato 7, 18, 37, 40, 45, 51, 74, 123, 124,
  125, 126n, 127, 128, 129
Plotinus 123, 128
pluralism 28
Poland 37
Poletown 79–81
pollution 26, 27, 62, 62n, 106, 111
Pols, Ed 2n
Popper, Karl 40–43, 45
positive externalities 111
Powell, Jim 60n
preemptive intervention 61
price support 9, 28
prior restraint 58, 60, 61n, 62, 62n
privacy 65
private property 3, 10–16, 22, 32–33, 43,
  55, 62, 80, 87, 96, 103, 105, 124
profit 3–5, 8, 18, 44, 72, 109, 110, 113, 118,
  124, 126
propaganda 80, 81
property 37
property laws 67, 68
property rights 12, 58, 59, 65, 68, 105
prosperity 3

Printed in the United States
97832LV00003B/337-339/A